The MONOCLE
Travel Guide Series

Tokyo

For more information,
please visit *gestalten.com*
———
Bibliographic information
published by the Deutsche
Nationalbibliothek: The Deutsche
Nationalbibliothek lists this publication in the Deutsche National-
bibliografie; detailed bibliographic
data are available online
at *dnb.d-nb.de*

This book was printed on
paper certified by the FSC®

Monocle editor in chief:
Tyler Brûlé
Monocle editor: *Andrew Tuck*
Series editor: *Joe Pickard*
Guide editor: *Fiona Wilson*
———
Designed by *Monocle*
Proofreading by *Monocle*
Typeset in *Plantin & Helvetica*
———
Printed by *Offsetdruckerei
Grammlich, Pliezhausen*

Made in Germany

Published by *Gestalten*, Berlin 2015
ISBN 978-3-89955-574-5

3rd printing, 2016

© Die Gestalten Verlag GmbH &
Co. KG, Berlin 2015

Welcome
—— Life beyond
the bright lights

At MONOCLE we love a *well-run city* and one capital that deserves that epithet more than any other is Tokyo. With its *clean streets*, *punctual transport* and *polite service* at every turn, the Japanese capital is the last word in efficiency. But its charms run so much deeper: in spite of its size – 13 million people live here – this city has *warmth* and *cosiness*. If Tokyo's reputation is that of an imposing, neon-lit modern realm, a visit will reveal a very different side: *low-rise*, *leafy* and *welcoming*.

For this travel guide our Tokyo editorial team has canvassed the metropolis for places that highlight this lesser-known side. We show a balance of the *old* and *new*, the *monumental* and *artisanal*. Many are our own favourite haunts: *one-man coffee shops*, *architectural gems* and neighbourhoods where you can *wander on foot* or *explore by bicycle* and find something surprising around every corner. We have compiled a list of the city's *best fashion retailers*, bars that make *superlative cocktails* and family-run restaurants specialising in *hearty meals* that the usual food guides might overlook.

You will notice that we have opted to leave out many of the obvious tourist spots in favour of shops, restaurants and parks that are dear to us. This is for those who want to immerse themselves in the *bountiful culture*, listen to some *J-pop*, grasp what lies beyond the big streets and neon lights and see how *traditional craftsmanship* has shaped *contemporary design*. — (M)

Contents
—— Navigating the city

Use the key below to help navigate the guide section by section.

 H Hotels

 F Food and drink

 R Retail

 T Things we'd buy

 E Essays

 C Culture

 D Design and architecture

 S Sport and fitness

 W Walks

Map
—— The city at a glance

Tokyo is a port city with no clear centre. It spans 23 wards, two rivers and heaps of landfill. Known as Edo during medieval times, the city has been standing since the mid-1400s and over the centuries has been shaped by natural disasters, war, changing technology and economic growth.

Much of what we focus on in these pages lies between Naka-meguro on the west side and Kiyosumi to the east. Many of Tokyo's retail areas are likely to be around for decades to come: the fashion stores in Aoyama, the record shops in Shinjuku, the old-school *yoshoku* (western-style cuisine) restaurants in Asakusa.

But more so than other cities, Tokyo is constantly reinventing itself. Use this map to explore and keep in mind that so much of what makes this metropolis special is hidden away on backstreets or in closet-sized spaces, often revealed during unexpected moments.

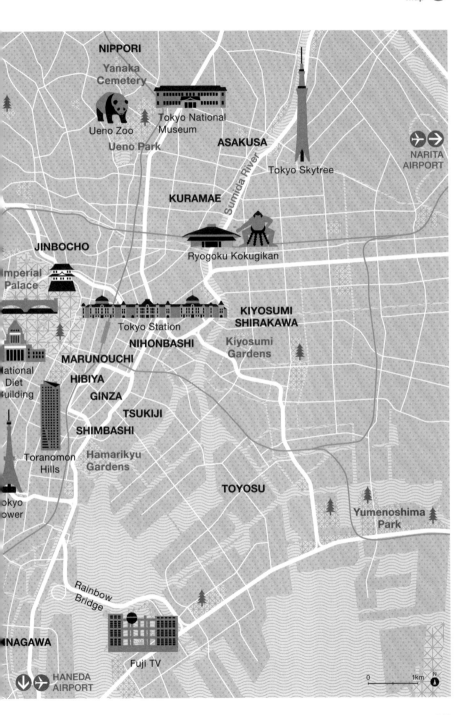

NIPPORI

Yanaka
Cemetery

Tokyo National
Museum

Ueno Zoo

Ueno Park

ASAKUSA

Tokyo Skytree

NARITA
AIRPORT

KURAMAE

Sumida River

JINBOCHO

Imperial
Palace

Ryogoku Kokugikan

Tokyo Station

KIYOSUMI
SHIRAKAWA

NIHONBASHI

Kiyosumi
Gardens

MARUNOUCHI

National
Diet
Building

HIBIYA

GINZA

TSUKIJI

SHIMBASHI

Toranomon
Hills

Hamarikyu
Gardens

TOYOSU

Tokyo
Tower

Yumenoshima
Park

NAGAWA

Rainbow
Bridge

Fuji TV

HANEDA
AIRPORT

0   1km   N

Need to know
—— Get to grips with the basics

From how to eat noodles to wearing the right socks, this is how to get off on the right foot in the Japanese capital. Learn some of the key Tokyo customs and good manners to help you fit in seamlessly (or at least avoid any unnecessary embarrassment).

City sticklers
Etiquette

Tokyo manages to avoid the chaos of other cities. How? Etiquette rules – but those rules aren't always obvious. When riding escalators you stand on the left and pass on the right. Don't cut to the front of a queue; be considerate and ask where it ends. Many streets and parks are now smoke-free so if you want to light up in public, look for ash bins in designated areas (or carry a pocket-sized ashtray). However, don't fret too much about breaking the rules; rarely will anyone shout or shoot dirty looks at you for an inadvertent violation.

Table manners
Chopsticks

Deftly handled, a pair of chopsticks can slice meat, separate fish flesh from bone and pick clean a bowl of rice. But having the skills is less important than knowing chopstick taboos. Rule one: it's rude to point the tips at anyone. Rule two: never leave chopsticks planted vertically in your rice (it's a funeral ritual). Rule three: never pass food with your chopsticks to someone else's (another funeral ritual). For less-than-confident users there's a fallback option: ask for a fork.

I'm sorry I pointed my chopsticks at you

Stand-up socks
Footwear

Dosoku de agaru describes the unpardonable act of entering a house with your shoes on. It should be obvious where to remove your footwear inside the front door. Some restaurants may also ask you to do so. If you want to avoid the embarrassment of padding around in socks with holes, stock up on a few new pairs before you arrive or head down to sock specialist Tabio.

Pay as you go
Money

These days many retailers accept touch-and-pay commuter cards. Yet a surprising number of restaurants and bars still stubbornly insist on old-fashioned cash. Carry plenty of money and don't worry about being robbed (it's highly unlikely). But you might need to try a few ATMS (including those at 7-Elevens and the post office) before you find one that will accept the cards that you use at home.

Cash out of hand
Paying

The money tray is a fixture of every taxi, supermarket, restaurant and clothing shop. It helps to ensure that bills and coins are properly accounted for and nobody gets short-changed. When paying, don't try handing money to the cashier: you will only be asked to place it in the tray. And don't worry about tipping for exceptional service; it's just not part of the culture.

Are you sure I can't offer you a tip for this?

All hail the cab
Transport

Tokyo's taxis are big on hospitality. Cars are spotless, seats come with embroidered covers and drivers are courteous. They even open and close the back door for you (from their seat) so don't try to slam it shut or even open it yourself. For the best service, flag down a black taxi. They cost the same as ordinary cabs but the drivers have worked hard to earn elite status in their fleets.

Noisy noodles
Eating

Slurping soba, ramen, somen or udon is standard practice. It takes skill to eat this way without choking or soiling the front of your favourite pressed Oxford shirt. But don't worry: this time your mother won't scold you. Occasionally you will witness someone – usually an office lady (or OL) – delicately eating noodles off a scoop-like spoon without making any noise; it's not impolite or wrong. But Japanese noodle connoisseurs will tell you that slurping is the only way to enjoy *nodogoshi*: the sensation as the strands wiggle and slide down your throat.

Safe and sound
Evening jingle

Every evening, as dusk approaches, you will hear a tune that lasts about 30 seconds. This is *Yuyake Koyake* (*Twilight*), and for decades it has functioned as a daily test of the emergency PA system. It also doubles as a reminder to children in parks and playgrounds that it's time to start heading home.

Box clever
Policing

In central Tokyo you're never far from a police box, or *koban*. Usually staffed by two police officers, the *koban* bring a sense of security to the city's streets. They have been a fixture in Japan since the 1870s and help prevent crime but their officers also direct traffic, give directions and can help track down a lost wallet. Look for police mascot Pipo-kun, a yellow mouse-like creature with an antenna whose name is a combination of "people" and "police", as well as referring to the sound of a siren.

Seasonal fare
Dining out

A handy word when dining out is *osusume*: recommendations. Menus at restaurants serving *washoku* (Japanese cuisine) constantly change to reflect what's in season. Ask the chef or waiter to suggest something that's only available now. And if you prefer to leave all the decisions to the chef simply say *omakase*: I'll leave it to you. You will rarely be disappointed.

Devil in the details
Business cards

When meeting someone for the first time, immediately reach for the case with your business cards. If you don't have a case, buy one. Exchanging name cards (*meishi kokan*) is just one of the many rituals of Japanese business culture and you will want to carry more than you know what to do with. When presenting your card, always use both hands and turn it so the type faces away from you. Body language is also an important part of introducing yourself. How you pass your card and receive the other person's might reflect where you are in the pecking order or how you view your own status. Everyone does it differently but you generally can't go wrong with the humble approach: a bend at the waist while presenting the card and a bow after the exchange. People look closely at the design and quality of paper so do invest in a decent stock. If you are coming to Japan on a regular basis it would be worth having your details printed on one side in Japanese. Treat any cards you are given with care: don't bend them in half or stick in a back pocket.

Yes, thanks, I am rather good. Would you like my business card?

Hotels
—— Hospitality at its finest

Twenty years ago the hotel scene in Tokyo was dominated by big Japanese names such as the Okura, the New Otani and the Imperial, the latter a stalwart of Tokyo hospitality since 1890. Then came the arrival, or so it seemed, of every major international hotel brand. Suddenly Tokyo has a Ritz-Carlton, Shangri-La, Four Seasons, Conrad and all the rest.

These places certainly deliver but it is hard not to feel affection for the Japanese classics. In a city where the hotels are as large as small towns, boutique venues have never taken off, although the Claska in Meguro has carved out its own niche in the market. The heavily used mid-range could still do with some work but top-end hotel arrivals continue apace: the Andaz opened in 2014, the long-awaited Aman a few months later. For the full Japanese hotel experience most visitors have to travel to a traditional *ryokan* inn outside the city, although from 2016 central Tokyo will have its first luxury Japanese-style hotel.

①
The Peninsula Tokyo, Hibiya
Luxury landmark

Tokyo has no shortage of luxury hotels but for location it's hard to beat the Peninsula. Standing on a corner in Hibiya this glossy landmark, which opened in 2007, is close to the busy districts of Ginza and Marunouchi and the stately gardens of the Imperial Palace. Service here is all about attention to detail and features the much-loved delivery-hatch system where guests can pile up dishes, unpolished shoes and laundry to be removed from the outside without the need to open their doors.

Fitness fiends will enjoy using the palace moat and grounds as a running track but the hotel also has a 24-hour gym, indoor pool and spa. The Peninsula is only a short hop from Tokyo Station and is well placed for Haneda Airport when it's time to make a getaway.
1-8-1 Yurakucho, Chiyoda-ku
+81 (0)3 6270 2888
tokyo.peninsula.com

MONOCLE COMMENT: The concierge team can arrange for some unusual outings including a trip to a saké brewery, an insider tour of the contemporary-art scene and personal shopping at the nearby Hankyu Men's department store, home of The Monocle Café.

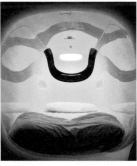

Nine Hours, Narita Airport
Scaled-down chic

With his first Nine Hours in Kyoto, Keisuke Yui reinvented the capsule hotel. For his second property, Yui chose Tokyo's Narita Airport. Each element in the 129-pod hotel has been chosen for its quality: the mattresses by 450-year-old company Nishikawa have been custom designed for comfort and ventilation; the pillows are made by top Nagoya manufacturer Kitamura; and the lightly fragranced silicon-free shower gel comes from Japanese brand Tamanohada.

Guests remove their shoes at check-in, leave luggage in a locker and slip into custom-developed nightwear before heading to a pristine sleep pod, which comes with dimmer switch and optional ambient sounds. The hotel – the only one inside the airport – is open 24 hours, with prices starting from a reasonable ¥1,500 for a two-hour nap.
Narita International Airport, Terminal 2
+81 (0)476 335 109
ninehours.co.jp/narita

MONOCLE COMMENT: If staying overnight, opt for the breakfast plan: for a few hundred extra yen you can enjoy the morning set at nearby Café de Crié.

peas in a pod
—
Nine Hours' capsules promote good sleep

If people can sleep in pods, why not owls in suitcases?

CUSTOMS

Things to know when checking in to a hotel room in Japan

01 Keep an eye on the time: Don't arrive too early. Check-in is usually at 14.00 and often 15.00 at a traditional *ryokan* inn. You could be left sitting in the lobby if you rock up in advance, which can be trying if you've come off a long flight. If you're concerned, ask if an early check-in is possible.

02 Smoke signals: If you're not a smoker be sure to ask for a no-smoking room, particularly in Japanese business hotels where windows don't open and the smell of stale cigarettes lingers. Smoking is still permitted in almost all Japanese hotels, bars and restaurants.

03 When bedding down: If you're hunting for your bed in a traditional *ryokan* with *tatami* mats, don't bother. The mattresses are neatly folded away in a cupboard during the day and will be laid out for you after dinner. No need to worry about sleeping on the floor either: the mats are soft and the futon mattresses comfortable.

04 Look the part: One of the pleasures of a Japanese hotel is the crisp *yukata* cotton robe that is almost certainly in a drawer in your room. In the winter there is also likely to be a warmer *haori* jacket to wear on top.

05 Watch your step: The slippers are there for a reason: they serve as a gentle reminder for you to remove your shoes. Take your cue from the Japanese home – no shoes indoors.

③
Hotel New Otani, Akasaka
Old-school opulence

Opened in 1964 in time for the Olympics, the Hotel New Otani waves the banner for early-1960s modernism. This sprawling hotel with multiple buildings, shopping malls and a large outdoor summer pool lies in a four-hectare site with a 400-year-old garden.

It's something of a blast from the past but its 1,479 rooms carry an unmistakable flavour of Tokyo. Sekishin-tei, a counter teppanyaki restaurant, offers a lovely dining experience from a small pavilion in the garden. James Bond fans might recognise the New Otani as the HQ for Osato Chemicals in the 1967 007 classic *You Only Live Twice*.
4-1 Kioi-cho, Chiyoda-ku
+81 (0)3 3265 1111
newotani.co.jp/tokyo

MONOCLE COMMENT: Opt for a main-building room with large windows and a garden view, then try whisked green tea in the authentic tea ceremony room, Seisei-An.

Catching butterflies? No, I'm just here to catch up on some sleep

Good morning
—
Both western and Japanese breakfasts are served

④

Mitsui Garden Hotel Ginza
Premier, Ginza
Mixing old and new

Ginza has changed dramatically over the past decade. Once the epitome of old-fashioned gentility, it has seen an influx of glossy luxury brands and towering flagships for the likes of Uniqlo. The old Ginza is still there though and it's an area that rewards exploration. The Mitsui Garden Ginza Premier is a good base, sat at the Shimbashi end and close to sushi shops, cocktail bars and *kissaten* coffee shops.

Priced in the mid-range, this recently renovated hotel starts at the 16th floor and has 361 rooms (45 with bathrooms with a view of Tokyo), a restaurant and a dimly lit counter bar that stays open until 02.00. There are some nice touches: the pillows come from Lofty, a well-known maker from nearby Nihonbashi. Unless you don't mind, ask for a no-smoking room.
8-13-1 Ginza, Chuo-ku
+81 (0)3 3543 1131
gardenhotels.co.jp/eng/ginza-premier

MONOCLE COMMENT: The hotel is just a few minutes' walk from Café de l'Ambre, one of Tokyo's oldest (and best) coffee shops. The owner, Ichiro Sekiguchi, is now a centenarian but is still in charge of the café's large roasting machine.

⑤

Grand Hyatt Tokyo, Roppongi
Hustle and bustle

One of the busiest hotels in Tokyo, the Grand Hyatt sits right on the edge of the giant Roppongi Hills development. Reliable, well situated and humming with activity, the hotel has 387 rooms, including 28 suites. For breakfast meetings or a weekend brunch head to The French Kitchen; for a heartier hit order a hefty steak and fries at The Oak Door. For anything in between try one of the hotel's several Japanese restaurants.
6-10-3 Roppongi, Minato-ku
+81 (0)3 4333 1234
tokyo.grand.hyatt.jp

MONOCLE COMMENT: Guests staying in Grand Club rooms get breakfast, evening cocktails and speedy check-in and check-out options – and they also have access to a spacious lounge, dedicated concierge services and free use of the Nagomi spa and fitness facilities as they see fit.

A grand bird deserves a grand hotel, I'd say
MONOCHAN

Suite dreams

The Grand Hyatt sits in Roppongi Hills, home to the Mori Art Museum, a multiplex cinema and dozens of shops, restaurants and apartments. The hotel's Presidential Suite occupies the entire 21st floor and is the only one in Tokyo to have its own private outdoor swimming pool.

(6)

Park Hyatt Tokyo, Shinjuku
Sky-high boutique

Now that many other international
chain hotels have made their mark
on Tokyo, it is easy to forget that
the Park Hyatt was one of the first.
More than two decades in, the
sky-rise luxury hotel remains a firm
favourite. Although the entrance
(along with a café-deli) is at
ground level, the rest occupies
the top floors of a Kenzo Tange-
designed skyscraper in Shinjuku.
There are 177 rooms, including
23 suites, but there always seems
to be a quiet hush in the corridors.

Popular with visiting celebrities,
the hotel has been a star in its own
right ever since featuring as the
setting for Sofia Coppola's film,
Lost in Translation. The New York
Grill and its bar on the 52nd floor
are consistently good and the hotel
has been meticulously maintained
and gently renovated over the years
to keep it fresh.

Rooms come with Aesop
bath products, crisp linens and
mesmerising views across Tokyo;
larger suites also have a carefully
chosen library of books. The gym
and swimming pool will encourage
anyone to exercise and the spa is
spectacular, with a good selection
of running shorts, thick robes and
jinbei pyjamas for guests to use.
3-7-1-2 Nishi Shinjuku, Shinjuku-ku
+81 (0)3 5322 1234
tokyo.park.hyatt.com

MONOCLE COMMENT: Views are an
obligatory feature of Tokyo hotels
and this one has some of the best.
If you want to wake up to Mount
Fuji, ask for a Park Deluxe room.

Above them all
—

Sky-high hotels atop office
towers are ubiquitous in
Tokyo nowadays but the
Park Hyatt was the first.
Perched on the 39th to
52nd floors of the Shinjuku
Park Tower, the hotel sits next
to the vast home of the Tokyo
Metropolitan Government,
known as Tocho.

Never mind 'Lost in Translation', I'm just plain lost

Bon appetit
—
The Girandole is styled after a French brasserie

Hoshinoya Tokyo

Most authentic *ryokan* inns in Tokyo are small, basic and away from the centre. That will change in 2016 with the opening of a new Japanese-style hotel in Marunouchi, the business centre of Tokyo. The Hoshinoya Tokyo will be the first of its kind in the city: a luxury 18-storey *ryokan* that will offer visitors the traditional experience – updated and adapted – that the capital has been lacking.

There will be *tatami* mats throughout (including the lifts), which means guests will be expected to remove their shoes on arrival as they would in any traditional inn. The hotel will have its own *onsen* bath on the top floor with spring water piped up from 1.5km below the property. Meanwhile, all the beds have been carefully designed to be as close to a traditional Japanese futon mattress as possible.

The company behind this ambitious project is Hoshino Resorts, run by Yoshiharu Hoshino, who hails from a family of Karuizawa hoteliers that stretches all the way back to 1904. On the company's website he hails the project as "a new operating model for urban hotels [that is] totally different from that of western-style hotels".
global.hoshinoresort.com

Famous friends
—
Celebrated novelist Yasunari Kawabata was the first writer to stay at the Hilltop and many followed: Shotaro Ikenami favoured room 401, while Hitomi Yamaguchi stayed in 403 each summer. Many rooms include antique writing desks if you find yourself in the mood to pen a haiku.

Yamanoue Hotel, Ochanomizu
Quirky and charismatic

The Hilltop Hotel – *Yama no ue* in Japanese – is a one-off. Founded in 1954 in a building from 1937 that was previously used by occupying US forces, the hotel sits on top of Surugadai Hill in Kanda. With Meiji University and dozens of bookshops nearby, the area has a strong intellectual bent and used to be frequented by writers such as Yukio Mishima.

The Hilltop can't boast luxury facilities but it has an old-fashioned charm that is increasingly rare. Regulars keep coming back for the popular tempura restaurant or to snack on Mont Blanc cakes in the busy coffee parlour. All the rooms have western-style beds but ask for a *washitsu* if you want *tatami* floors and *shoji* screens. This hotel may not be for those who are looking for international five-star luxury but it's refreshingly different.
1-1 Kanda Surugadai, Chiyoda-ku
+81 (0)3 3293 2311
yamanoue-hotel.co.jp

MONOCLE COMMENT: The garden rooms are best – they come with a small patch of green – while the Mozart room at the very top of the hotel has giant vintage speakers and a sound system for classical-music fans.

I'm bored. Time to head to the Royal Bar

(8)

Palace Hotel Tokyo, Marunouchi
State-of-the-art renovation

Loyal customers at the Palace
Hotel feared that the essential
atmosphere of the 1961 original
would be lost when it was torn
down and rebuilt from scratch.
They needn't have worried.

Yes, the new 290-room hotel
that was unveiled in 2012 is
sparkling and modern: the sunny
rooms with their generous
bathrooms and Japanese bed linen
are a major upgrade; the Evian spa
is a state-of-the-art retreat; and the
moat-side terrace and lobby lounge
are smart additions. But the feel
of the old place is still there. The
hotel's Japanese identity is never
forgotten, from the highly rated
restaurants to the shopping arcade,
which has been filled with an
imaginative selection of Japanese
products and handicrafts.

Most of the staff from the old
hotel returned, including Masaru
Watanabe (*pictured*), the charming
GM. Other welcome returnees
include the dimly lit Royal Bar
and the Michelin-starred French
restaurant Crown, long favoured
by politicos from nearby
Kasumigaseki. And, of course,
that thrilling view over the
Imperial Palace.
*1-1-1 Marunouchi, Chiyoda-ku
+81 (0)3 3211 5211
palacehoteltokyo.com*

MONOCLE COMMENT: For lunch or
dinner with a view book a private
tatami room at the Wadakura
kaiseki restaurant. Try the house
saké 1-1-1, made for the hotel by
famed Niigata brewer Hakkaisan.

Old school

The Palace
knows how to
do luxury

9

Mandarin Oriental Tokyo,
Nihonbashi
For the dedicated diner

Nihonbashi, a more traditional
district, has undergone a facelift
in recent years and the Mandarin
Oriental's arrival in 2005 was part
of it. The hotel has all the luxury
you would expect: 178 generous
rooms (with 21 suites), a scenic spa
and 12 restaurants – including three
(French, Cantonese and molecular)
that each have a Michelin star – and
an eight-seater sushi restaurant with
a 350-year-old cypress counter.
   Be sure to drop in on the nearby
Coredo buildings for restaurants and
shops, including knife specialist
Kiya, in business since 1792.
*2-1-1 Nihonbashi Muromachi,
Chuo-ku
+81 (0)3 3270 8800
mandarinoriental.com/tokyo*

MONOCLE COMMENT: Try chief
bartender Yukiyo Kurihara's
Nihonbashi cocktail with vodka,
yuzu liqueur, grapefruit juice and
a spiral of lime.

10

Cerulean Tower Tokyu
Hotel, Shibuya
Centrally located convenience

For a prime tourist destination,
Shibuya has always been short on
quality hotels. The Cerulean has
been filling that gap since 2001 in
a tower close to the centre of the
action and minutes from Shibuya
Station. There are 411 rooms,
including nine suites and two
Japanese rooms. The rooms are
between the 19th and 37th floors
and there are good views over
the city – even better from the
40th-floor bar and restaurant. This
hotel even has its own *Noh* theatre
where performances of Japan's
most esoteric dramatic art are held.
*26-1 Sakuragaokacho, Shibuya-ku
+81 (0)3 3476 3000
ceruleantower-hotel.com*

MONOCLE COMMENT: Book the
spacious 19th-floor *washitsu*: a
traditional room with a wooden
bath. The turndown service
involves laying out the futon
mattresses and quilts on the floor.

11

The Capitol Hotel Tokyu,
Nagata-cho
A Japanese legacy

There was sadness when a Tokyo classic, the Capitol Tokyu hotel in Akasaka, closed its doors in 2006 after 43 years. The Beatles stayed here in the 1960s and well-coiffed former prime minister Junichiro Koizumi was a regular at the hotel's barber. But after being redeveloped the hotel rose again in 2010 in a new incarnation designed by Kengo Kuma.

Housed within a 29-storey tower, the 251-room hotel retained its distinctly Japanese identity, albeit in a more minimalist guise. Kuma surrounded the hotel with water and greenery while the rooms channel the muted palette and textures of traditional Japan. Political heavyweights, who love the hotel's proximity to the Diet parliamentary building, also have a discreet venue for political intrigue in Suiren, the Japanese restaurant.
*2-10-3 Nagata-cho, Chiyoda-ku
+81 (0)3 3503 0109
capitolhoteltokyu.com/en*

MONOCLE COMMENT: The Capitol is next to Hie Shrine, a Shinto shrine that hosts the *Sanno Matsuri*: one of the three big festivals of Edo (Tokyo's old name). Bombed in the war, the old shrine was replaced with the current building in 1958.

Fresh start
——
The hotel was revamped after 43 years of business

Food and drink
—— Smart bites and top stops

It's not only sushi chefs and *kaiseki* specialists – celebrated defenders of traditional Japanese cuisine – who deserve mentioning in Tokyo. The variety of things to eat in this city will surprise you: from *tonkatsu* (deep-fried breaded pork) and soba (buckwheat noodles) to pizzas and steaks, you will find that even the most humble dishes are made to meticulous perfection. It's no surprise that Tokyo has earned more Michelin stars than any other city in the world.

But even if you choose not to indulge in the city's best restaurants you will not be disappointed. In this section we highlight our favourite *izakaya* gastropubs, the best spots for breakfast and the coffee shops where you will feel at home. You will find small bistros and bento shops, ramen and sweets vendors, teahouses and bars. Be prepared to eat well.

Restaurants
Rice, ramen and rare cuts

①
Akomeya Tokyo, Ginza
With the grain

What do sushi and saké have in common? Rice – that most versatile of crops. In Japan it's steamed, milled, brewed, distilled and pounded, ending up in cakes and condiments. Few shops showcase this better than Akomeya, opened in 2013 by Japanese retail group Sazaby League. It is also filled with 6,000 food and household products, including earthenware pots made in Saga, bamboo bento boxes, Tembea canvas bags and aprons by Minä Perhonen. The café offers light Japanese meals and at night the bar hosts saké tastings.
2-2-6 Ginza, Chuo-ku
+81 (0)3 6758 0271
akomeya.jp

③
Il Tamburello, Ningyocho
Upper crust

Neapolitan pizza is a deceptively simple dish that is hard to get right. One *pizzaiolo* who makes perfect margherita, *diavola* and *bianco* pizzas every time is Yoshihisa Otsubo (*pictured*). Since opening Il Tamburello in a former warehouse space in 2010, Otsubo has gone to great lengths to recreate the meals he spent three years making while training in Naples and Calabria. He shapes dough made from Molino Caputo flour that has spent a day rising before adding Salerno tomatoes and mozzarella from Caserta. The pizza then spends about one minute inside a 450c wood-fired stove made in Italy.

Otsubo's lunch menu is limited to half a dozen pizzas but at dinnertime his team has an extensive menu of them, plus antipasti platters and wines.
1-2-9 Nihonbashi-horidomecho, Chuo-ku
+81 (0)3 6661 6628
il-tamburello.com

②
New York Bar and Grill, Shinjuku
Fine cuts

Who could ever tire of the view from the New York Bar and Grill? Tokyo is laid out before diners on the 52nd floor of the luxury Park Hyatt Tokyo. The menu is rock solid – this is a good chance to try some top Kobe prime cut or Sendai tenderloin – and the dense Californian wine list is one of the largest in Japan. Even if you're not eating in the restaurant, a drink at the famous bar makes the trip worthwhile. A cocktail, the live music and those twinkling lights outside never fail to thrill.
52F, Park Hyatt Tokyo, 3-7-1-2 Nishi Shinjuku, Shinjuku-ku
+81 (0)3 5323 3458
tokyo.park.hyatt.com

From here I get a great view – of the bar

Three more

01 Da Babbo, Ningyocho: A few blocks away from Il Tamburello, chef Hideaki Okuno makes extraordinary pizzas, homemade gelato and antipasti to complement his selection of about 60 Italian wines.
da-babbo.jp

02 Pizzeria e Trattoria da Isa, Naka-meguro: Anyone still suffering from pizza withdrawal should head to two-time World Pizza Cup champion Hisanori Yamamoto's restaurant near Naka-meguro. Its variety (more than two dozen) and flavours rival the best in Naples.
da-isa.jp

03 Luccanalu, Uehara: More than a pizzeria, this 16-seat restaurant serves a classic margherita but steak and homemade sausages, too. There is also a fine range of biodynamic wines from which to choose.
luccanalu.jp

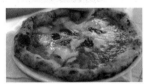

Must-try
Farm-to-table cooking from Eatrip, Harajuku

Yuri Nomura's Eatrip is the kind of restaurant that tells you who picked your beetroot and which farmer raised the pig that you're eating. Since opening in 2012, Nomura's farm-to-table menu and her love of combining travel and cooking in far-flung locales has helped spread her philosophy about eating well beyond the confines of her small restaurant near Harajuku.

Nomura, who did a stint at Chez Panisse in Berkeley, California, has played a key part in a new wave of cooking in Tokyo. Her restaurant, which is set in a snug wooden house with a small garden, is the last thing you'd expect to find just a few steps from crowded Omotesando.
6-31-10 Jingumae, Shibuya-ku
+81 (0)3 3409 4002
restaurant-eatrip.com

④
Okomeya, Togoshi
New neighbourhood hub

Its name translates as "rice shop" but as generic as that sounds, there's nothing ordinary about this retail space in a ceramic-tiled building on Togoshi's main street. Opened in 2014 by branding agency Owan and designed by Jo Nagasaka of Schemata Architects, Okomeya sells *onigiri* rice balls made from Koshihikari rice grown in Niigata.

Said delicacies help sell bags of rice but that is only part of what Owan is hoping to achieve. The firm, which has also started a café and coffee roastery in the area, wants to revive this empty, rundown strip.
4-3-2 Togoshi, Shinagawa-ku
+81 (0)3 6426 9601
owan.jp

⑤
Sahsya Kanetaka, Omotesando
Calm oasis

This Japanese restaurant in the Oak Omotesando building is located on one of the busiest shopping streets in Tokyo but head up to the second floor and the noise dissipates. The serene room with a 13-metre-wide picture window has a long table and another raised counter facing a small garden. The set lunch menu allows diners to pick from a selection that might include a *shabu shabu* hot pot with *Sangen* pork, *mizuna* leaf and citrus sauce or steamed trout sushi.
2F, Oak Omotesando,
3-6-1 Kita Aoyama, Minato-ku
+81 (0)3 6450 5116
kanetanaka.co.jp

Ginza Maru, Ginza
Lunchtime favourite

When Keiji Mori opened his restaurant Maru in Aoyama more than a decade ago he surprised Tokyo diners with his brand of casual Kyoto cooking. His fans' only complaint was that it didn't open for lunch; Mori solved that problem by opening another Maru in Ginza that serves lunch and dinner.

The lunch menu features dishes such as chicken *nabe* and yellowtail with a light teriyaki sauce and is exceptionally good value. Mori sources the best seasonal ingredients and even the standard elements of a Japanese meal – the rice, pickles and miso soup – are superior. The atmosphere at dinner is relaxed but don't be deceived: this is seriously good cooking.
*2F, Ichigo Ginza 612 Building,
6-12-15 Ginza, Chuo-ku
+81 (0)3 5537 7420
maru-mayfont.jp*

Curry cravings
—

It might come as a surprise that curry rice – 'kare raisu' – is Japanese comfort food. Recipes date back to the country opening up from isolation in the late 19th century. Every café and company canteen now has its own original recipe.

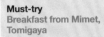

Must-try
Breakfast from Mimet, Tomigaya

At his café on the ground floor of a renovated 1970s wooden building, Taro Yamamoto has brought the breakfast culture of his hometown Nagoya to the capital: thick white toast, homemade jam, boiled eggs and coffee. Upstairs the shop has *nambu-tekki* ironware and French homeware, all chosen by Yamamoto's wife Ikumi. Mimet, which serves lunches and dinners too, is a short stroll from Yamamoto's two other bistros: Aruru and Urura share the same comfortable vibe.
puhura.co.jp

⑦
Ningyocho Imahan, Ningyocho
For contemporary carnivores

There are many excellent *sukiyaki* restaurants in Tokyo but Ningyocho Imahan is a classic. Founded in 1895, Imahan is set in a wooden building in the neighbourhood of Ningyocho, a short stroll from a busy Shinto shrine and the Meijiza *kabuki* theatre. Imahan is a family beef business and the menu – featuring teppanyaki, *shabu shabu* and *sukiyaki* – is not for vegetarians.

Head chef Kazuo Noguchi, who has been at Imahan for 30 years, knows how to prepare beef. The quality of the meat is key: Japanese wagyu is the order of the day, preferably from female black-haired cows. One thing to note with regards *sukiyaki*: it's pronounced *ski-yaki* not *sooky-yaki*. The word was hijacked for the English version of a Japanese hit song back in the 1960s and has been mispronounced ever since.
2-9-12 Nihonbashi Ningyocho, Chuo-ku
+81 (0)3 3666 7006
imahan.com

Bread boom
——
Not long ago, bread in Japan was just 'shoku-pan': the bland, blockish, spongy industrial-made variety. Now it is as easy to find neighbourhood bakeries across Tokyo that are making baguettes, 'pain de campagne' and fruit-and-nut loaves.

⑨ Yanmo, Aoyama
Strength in seafood

Only in Tokyo would you queue for fish. At this fixture of the capital's Aoyama district, customers come for the seafood brought in daily from the ports of Japan's Izu Peninsula. Yanmo has been serving up seasonal fish in this location for more than two decades. The best deals are to be had at lunchtime, when the superb mackerel is served salted or slightly fermented with a coating of Saikyo miso. And you can't go wrong with the *menuke* (red rockfish), a tender white-fleshed fish that is at its fatty prime in winter.
B1F, 5-5-25 Minami Aoyama, Minato-ku
+81 (0)3 5466 0636
yanmo.co.jp/aoyama

⑧ Kagari, Ginza
Small and perfectly formed

The lunchtime queue in front of this eight-seat restaurant in a Ginza alleyway may leave you wondering why there is so much fuss over a bowl of noodles. The answer is that the ramen here (called *chuka* soba, hence the "Soba" sign outside) is nothing like the standard pork-based stuff that you will find elsewhere.

Kagari's *tori-paitan* soba comes with an ivory-coloured broth made from chicken and topped with thin chicken slices and seasonal vegetables, while its *niboshi-shoyu* soba is darker and made with dried sardines and soy sauce. The noodles are thin and firm and the toppings are an odd mix: soft-boiled egg, roast-beef slices, *sudachi* citrus and shallots. There is also a delicious *tokusei-tsukesoba* that is perfect for a hot summer's day. Despite its tiny dimensions, this dining spot is one of the highlights of the city's ramen scene.
Ginza A Building, 4-4-1 Ginza, Chuo-ku

⑩ Chaco Amemiya, Sendagaya
Sensational steaks

Michio Amemiya opened his popular steak restaurant in Sendagaya back in 1979. Today he runs the place with his two sons, Toshio and Ryota. Chunky steaks are cooked on a charcoal grill by the entrance to the restaurant, which infuses the room – and tempts passers-by – with inviting smells.

The dinner menu features premium cuts of Australian and Japanese beef, which includes the tenderest wagyu. The house style at Chaco Amemiya is to grill the meat lightly with a sprinkle of salt before transferring it to a hot cast-iron plate at the table. They don't skimp on the portions here: you can have your fillet steak with a baked potato, hearty salad and selection of cooked vegetables. Enjoy with a heavy Chilean red or a glass of Rubaiyat from the Marufuji winery in Yamanashi.
B1F, 1-7-12 Sendagaya, Shibuya-ku
+81 (0)3 3402 6066
homepage1.nifty.com/chaco

Must-try
Traditional breakfast from Yakumo-Saryo, Meguro

There is no better place for a traditional Japanese breakfast than Yakumo-Saryo on the city's west side. Don't expect bacon and eggs, though: your first meal of the day is likely to include white rice, miso soup, *himono* (semi-dried fish), pickles and *konbu tsukudani*, a soy-sauce-stewed kelp dish.

Created by design firm Simplicity, Yakumo-Saryo resembles a villa: it has a well-kept garden, split-level dining rooms and antique wooden furniture. In the tea salon a sommelier selects the green and roasted teas. The Japanese *wagashi* desserts (with *azuki* bean filling or sprinkled with sweet roasted soybean flour) are made by hand every day.
yakumosaryo.jp

⑪
Beard, Meguro
Simple charm

Small, convivial and reliably good,
Beard has been drawing diners to
a quiet street in Meguro since it
opened in 2012. Owner-chef Shin
Harakawa (*pictured*) – usually to
be found in a Breton shirt – is the
consummate host, chatting and
cooking at the same time. Although
Harakawa describes his culinary
style as "simple food with quality
ingredients", he is being modest.
His cooking has been honed at
a Michelin-starred restaurant in
Sens, France, and Chez Panisse
in Berkeley.

The refreshingly short menu is
likely to feature a tasty steak and
chips, fresh fish and imaginative
salads, made all the better for using
vegetables from farmers' markets
and meat that comes either direct
from farms or a trusted supplier.
Barely a dozen diners fit into the
small room, which is always buzzing
with chatter and well-chosen music.

On Sundays, Harakawa opens
for brunch – a rarity in Tokyo – and
serves ricotta pancakes, eggs and
burgers. Harakawa enjoys what
he does and it shows; Beard is the
neighbourhood restaurant every
city should have.
1-17-22 Meguro, Meguro-ku
+81 (0)3 5496 0567
b-e-a-r-d.com

⑫
Down the Stairs, Aoyama
Stepping out

Sonya Park, the founder of lifestyle
brand Arts & Science, originally
envisaged Down the Stairs as a
canteen for the staff of her clothing,
shoe and accessory shops upstairs;
luckily she realised her customers
would love it, too. The restaurant is
barely more than an open kitchen,
two wooden tables and a counter
with seats enough for 14.

At lunchtime healthy meals of
curries and salads are served, made
from a range of ingredients that
change with the seasons. There is
pleasure in sitting among the items
and materials that Park has selected
to furnish Down the Stairs: worn
wooden tables, concrete floors,
glassware by Kazumi Tsuji and
salt-fired ceramics by potter Steve
Harrison. Look out for the Supper
Club events hosted by visiting
chefs, too.
110 Palace Aoyama, 6-1-6 Minami
Aoyama, Minato-ku
+81 (0)3 5464 3711
arts-science.com

⑬ Toraya, Akasaka
Sweet dreams

This family-run confectioner has been around since the 16th century. Firm favourites include the *yokan* sweet-bean paste blocks, *monaka azuki* bean-filled wafers and *namagashi* pounded rice and cakes made with refined sugar from Kagawa and Tokushima.
4-9-22 Akasaka, Minato-ku
+81 (0)3 3408 4121
toraya-group.co.jp

⑭ Miyakawa, Aoyama
Tempura time

Miyakawa chef Isao Kanemasa (*pictured*) has been frying tempura in the same 18-seat shop in Aoyama since 1969. At lunchtime he stands at the counter dipping shrimp, seasonal vegetables, eel and Japanese whiting into flour and batter before dropping each one into a cast-iron pot of cotton-seed and sesame oil.

Kanemasa's batter is delightfully thin and crunchy and he recommends that customers use only salt for seasoning – Osaka-style – although he does also provide the traditional dipping sauce, radish and grated ginger.
6-1-6 Minami Aoyama, Minato-ku
+81 (0)3 3400 3722

⑮ Namikibashi Nakamura, Shibuya
Seasonal sensation

With so many *izakaya* to choose from, how do you decide which one to go to? Teiji Nakamura's Namikibashi Nakamura is one option where both the food and saké are always excellent.

The menu is seasonal and changes every month – *nanohana* topped with spicy miso and flying-fish sashimi in spring, for instance – and the staff are experts at recommending saké to complement the meal. Look for the lamp at the top of a set of stairs where you'll step through a heavy sliding door.
2F-B, Ipse Shibuya, 3-13-5 Shibuya, Shibuya-ku
+81 (0)3 6427 9580
ameblo.jp/fg-nakamura

⑯ Pignon, Kamiyama-cho
Fusion with finesse

This popular bistro was among the first newcomers to the MONOCLE bureau's Tomigaya neighbourhood, a short hop from Omotesando and Shibuya and a couple of blocks from Yoyogi Park.

Run by owner-chef Rimpei Yoshikawa and his small team, Pignon represents a new style of Tokyo cooking: casual and seasonal by way of California and France, with a hint of the spices of Moroccan cuisine. It's hard to pick favourites but Yoshikawa's Kumamoto Amakusa pork roast and miso-marinated foie gras are sensational.
16-3 Kamiyama-cho, Shibuya-ku
+81 (0)3 3468 2331

Must-try
Yoshuku from Shiseido Parlour, Ginza

Shiseido Parlour got its start in 1902 when it was merely a soda fountain in a pharmacy. Since then it has stuck to what it does best: Japanese-style western cuisine, known as *yoshoku*, that came into vogue in the late 19th century and is still available all over Tokyo. Here it is served by waiters in crisp shirts and bow ties who will make salads from scratch at a cart wheeled to your table. There are croquettes, *omu-rice*, curries, pilafs, hashed beef and other classics. This restaurant is old-school Ginza and the presentation follows suit with white Noritake porcelain and heavy cutlery from Christofle.
parlour.shiseido.co.jp

Healthy options

01 **Three, Aoyama:** Expect raw food, gluten-free dishes and cold-pressed juices at the café that Japanese skincare and cosmetics brand Three opened next to its shop and spa in Aoyama in 2013. Chef Keiko Hosoi's menu is seasonal and the gluten-free bread, pasta and other lunchtime options arrive with plenty of organic vegetables. This is also one of the few places in the city that opens early for breakfast.
aoyama.threecosmetics. com

02 **Sky High, Aoyama:** The juicing trend has yet to take off in Japan but this small bar is leading the way. The extensive menu runs from sweet fruit blends to iron-rich green juices and targets skin, blood and low energy; if you're in real need of a detox, Sky High will set up a five-day juice cleanse for you.
skyhigh-tokyo.jp

03 **Mominoki House, Harajuku:** Chef Eiichiro Yamada is one of the pioneers of Tokyo's organic, macrobiotic movement, producing menus that are healthy and satisfyingly tasty. Don't be shy about asking for help reading the daily specials written in Japanese on the blackboard.
2-18-5 Jingumae, Shibuya-ku

⑰
Ekibenya Matsuri, Tokyo Station
Box clever

What better way to pass the time on the Shinkansen than with an all-star bento box? Tokyo Station's Ekibenya Matsuri sells more than 170 varieties of *ekiben* (from the words for station and bento); takeaway meals are artfully arranged with an ever-changing assortment of local produce, fish and meat that is shipped in daily from around the country. There is *takomeshi* with octopus from Hyogo, grilled beef from Yamagata and *iwashi-kabayaki* (sardines) from Aomori. You will wonder why you ever bothered with sandwiches.
Tokyo Station, Central Street concourse
+81 (0)3 3213 4352
nre.co.jp

⑱
Ginza Akebono, Ginza
Crackers and candies

Ginza Akebono's flagship *okashi* (sweets and rice crackers) shop opened in 1948, at a time when sugar was hard to come by in Japan. That shop, in the heart of Ginza, has become a nationwide chain that is now led by the founder's granddaughter, Kayo Hosono. Known for its *kuri-monaka wagashi* sweets – filled with candied-chestnut and sweet-bean paste – and rice-cracker box-sets, Ginza Akebono has cultivated a broad fan base: CEOs, upscale *ryotei* restaurants and families buy the firm's products as gifts or treats.

In 2012 Hosono hired the Kyoto-based designer Hisanobu Tsujimura to redo the Ginza shop, which now features handmade ceramic floor tiles and wood-and-paper screens in a willow pattern covering the walls.
5-7-19 Ginza, Chuo-ku
+81 (0)3 3571 3640
ginza-akebono.co.jp

Sushi
Tokyo's top stops

(19)
Arms Burger, Yoyogi
Parkside patties

You might think Japan is all about
healthy eating but Tokyo chefs also
know how to serve a mean burger.
This place by Yoyogi Park does
some of the best, serving them in
a small restaurant that is rammed
at the weekend. You can also
get takeaway.
5-64-7 Yoyogi, Shibuya-ku
+81 (0)3 3466 5970
arms-burger.com

(20)
La Bettola da Ochiai, Ginza
Welcoming Italian

La Bettola da Ochiai is an Italian
restaurant on a quiet street in
Higashi Ginza. The exterior reveals
very little but open the door and
you will find a busy team of waiters
serving Italian food to a full house:
grilled tuna and fresh-fish carpaccio
and a variety of home-cooked
pastas, including a rich beef-cheek
rigatoni and creamy lasagne.

Chef Tsutomu Ochiai, who
opened the restaurant in 1997, grew
up in Tokyo but spent three years
in Italy working his way through
numerous kitchens. Today he has
branches in Nagoya and Toyama
but the original Ginza restaurant
is cheery and unpretentious. The
dolce menu is extensive but if you
still want more crème caramel or
tiramisu, go up the road to the
Dolce La Bettola shop. That's where
the bread, tarts and cakes are baked;
there's a small hatch for takeaways.
1-21-2 Ginza, Chuo-ku
+81 (0)3 3567 5656
la-bettola.co.jp

(1)
Midori Sushi, Shibuya
Chain with charm

Tokyo has thousands of sushi
restaurants, from chain shops that
use conveyor belts to the most
celebrated establishments (some
with strict rules about who gets in).
Price often dictates quality and
where to go for the best sushi is
a matter of debate.

For an unfussy, satisfying meal
try Umegaoka Sushi no Midori
in Shibuya. At lunchtime this
casual restaurant's Ultimate Sushi
Assortment is a popular choice:
fatty tuna, shrimp, eel, urchin
and a few seasonal specialities. The
portions are sizeable and the fish
reliably fresh, and diners with
a big appetite can ask for larger
shari: the oval balls of rice beneath
the fish. Avoid peak times or be
prepared to wait for an hour.
Umegaoka Sushi no Midori has
10 locations around Tokyo.
*4F, Mark City, 1-12-3 Dogenzaka
Shibuya-ku*
+81 (0)3 5458 0002
sushinomidori.co.jp

Two more

01 Tsukiji Sushiko, Tsukiji:
A Tokyo sushi chain that
has its flagship shop
a few blocks from the
Tsukiji fish market,
Tsukiji Sushiko is reliably
tasty with prices that
are mid-range. A big
catch, such as the
record-breaking 400kg
bluefin tuna from a fishing
port in western Japan in
2013, can attract a crush
of diners.
tsukiji-sushiko.com

02 Sushi Tsubaki, Ginza:
This small Ginza
restaurant with a spartan
interior is a practitioner
of the Edomae sushi
tradition that dates back
to the early 1800s. It is
so close to Tsukiji fish
market that the chefs
pedal over to find out
what has been freshly
caught every morning.
The classic presentation
is simple, the execution
is flawless and the
ambience is relaxed.
sushitsubaki.jp

Soba
Noodle nirvana

Teuchisoba Narutomi, Tsukiji
Smooth operator

Masaaki Narutomi makes his soba
only from buckwheat flour, which
explains the noodles' delicious
aroma and smooth texture. If
you pay a visit, don't miss the
uni-tsukudani (salted, dried sea
urchin) and the *gobo* tempura
(burdock root).
8-18-6 Ginza, Chuo-ku
+81 (0)3 5565 0055
narutomi-soba.net

Three more

**01 Edo Soba Hosokawa,
Ryogoku:** Tadashi
Hosokawa's fragrant soba
and delicious starters –
anago (conger-eel)
tempura and *tamago-yaki*
(omelette) – attract diners
from afar. Such is
Hosokawa's reputation
that many of the city's
most talented soba
artisans train here.
edosoba-hosokawa.jp

02 Itasoba Kaoriya, Ebisu:
On Tokyo's west side,
Kaoriya in Ebisu feeds
a steady stream of
customers at communal
tables until midnight. This
restaurant's trademark
chewy soba comes in two
sizes – thick and thicker –
and its familiar side dishes
of tempura, fish cakes
and grilled miso paste
are made to perfection.
*foodgate.net/
shop_kaoriya.html*

03 Kyorakutei, Kagurazaka:
Kyorakutei makes soba
from 100 per cent
buckwheat flour that
is stone-milled on the
premises. The light, crispy
tempura is almost as
big a draw as the soba.
Depending on the season
you might get eggplant
and *shishito* peppers.
kyourakutei.com

①
Tamawarai, Jingumae
Bucking the trend

Masahiro Arakawa (*pictured*) is
one of the city's most revered
artisans of soba: noodles made
from buckwheat. At his restaurant,
which he opened in 2010, he
mills about 5kg of buckwheat
daily from eight farms in Ibaraki,
and some from his own fields
in Tochigi. Urakawa turns this
coarse-ground buckwheat
flour into soba noodles that he
serves cold (*zaru*-soba) with an
umami-packed *tsuyu* broth made
from shaved bonito. His portions
are small but that's intentional:
any more and the noodles would
sit too long and lose their firmness.
    The Kyushu *kuruma-ebi* he
grills has been marinated in a
sweet, savoury Saikyo miso paste
for three days and he serves
herring that has simmered for six
days. Try the *dashi-maki tamago*, a
scrambled-egg dish that is a soba
restaurant standard. Urakawa's
saké list features rare finds,
including Rikuyu from the
mountains of Kyoto and Higan
from Niigata. When it's cold
outside he adds *soba-yu* – the
viscous water that the soba
noodles have been boiled in –
to shochu, a distilled tipple.
5-23-3 Jingumae, Shibuya-ku
+81 (0)3 5485 0025

Tonkatsu
Bread of heaven

① Butagumi, Nishi Azabu
Pork perfection

Purists will tell you to head to Butagumi for the best *tonkatsu* (breaded pork cutlet) in Tokyo. The restaurant – an old two-storey wooden house – is run by chef Satoshi Oishi (*pictured*). It's all about the pork: choose from around 50 varieties, including *kurobuta* (Berkshire) from Kagoshima and *hakkinton* (Berkshire, Yorkshire and Landrace crossbreed) from Iwate; or, from more distant shores, Mangalica from Hungary and Iberico from Spain. For the indecisive there's the Butagumi-zen, a sampler set of bite-sized *tonkatsu*.
2-24-9 Nishi Azabu, Minato-ku
+81 (0) 5466 6775
butagumi.com

② Maisen, Omotesando
Global reputation

Don't let the fact that Maisen is popular with tourists put you off: it makes consistently flawless tonkatsu. Founded by housewife Chiyoko Koide back in 1965, it now has nine restaurants and dozens of outlets in department stores and train stations. This, the flagship, has the best ambience.
4-8-5 Jingumae, Shibuya-ku
mai-sen.com

③ Ginza Bairin, Ginza
Tokyo classic

Ginza Bairin, a family-run business in Ginza, has been making *tonkatsu* and *katsudon* (pork cutlet with scrambled egg on rice) since 1927. Founder Nobukatsu Shibuya invented the *hito-kuchi* (bite-sized) cutlet and a sauce that derives its sweetness from apples.
7-8-1 Ginza, Chuo-ku
+81 (0)3 3571 0350
ginzabairin.com

Coffee
Fine morning fixes

①

Kissaten, citywide
A local experience

Before anyone had thought of
Starbucks, Japan had its *kissaten*, or
coffee shops. There are thousands
of them: smoky station pit stops,
literary *bundan kissa* lined with
books, jazz *kissa*, and *meikyoku
kissa*: classical-music cafés where
patrons sit in silence and listen
to the music. The atmosphere,
and frequently the interiors, are a
throwback that shouldn't be missed.

Three more

01 **Cafe de l'Ambre, Ginza:**
Centenarian Ichiro
Sekiguchi opened his café
in Ginza in 1948 and is
still working here. Coffee-
lovers come for the
master's cloth-filtered brew.
h6.dion.ne.jp/~lambre

02 **Stone, Yurakucho:** Office
workers have been coming
to Stone since 1966.
Order a *fruits-sando*:
a sandwich made with
white bread, cream,
pineapple and banana.
+81 (0)3 3213 2651

03 **Lawn, Yotsuya:** Expect a
pristine 1960s interior and
a fine milk coffee served
by owner Hiroaki Ogura.
The milkshake is made
the old way with raw egg
and fresh lemon.
*yama.ne.jp/yotsuya/shop/
lown/index.html*

②

Onibus Coffee Nakameguro,
Meguro
Skilled touch

A former carpenter, Atsushi
Sakao got hooked on coffee
when he was backpacking in
Australia and founded his first
coffee shop in Okusawa in 2012.
This coffee shop next to a park
behind Nakameguro Station
opened four years later. Sakao
takes a hands-on approach: he
meets the farmers, roasts the
beans and makes the coffee. Sit
on a bench outside or enjoy the
view of cherry blossoms from
upstairs. Sakao also runs About
Life Coffee in Shibuya.
*2-14-1 Kamimeguro, Meguro-ku
+81 (0)3 6412 8683
onibuscoffee.com*

③
Coffeehouse Nishiya, Shibuya
Personal service

Coffeehouse Nishiya's resemblance to a neighbourhood bar in Italy is no coincidence. Kyohei Nishiya has gone to great lengths to achieve it (right down to the waistcoat and long apron) but everything he knows he picked up while training at restaurants and cafés in Tokyo. His repertoire includes *caffe con panna*, Irish coffee and espresso *shakerato*, along with the usual espresso and milk varieties.

In a big and busy city such as Tokyo you wouldn't necessarily expect the barista to remember your personal preferences after just a handful of visits – but that is exactly the kind of thing that happens at Coffeehouse Nishiya.
1-4-1 Higashi, Shibuya-ku
+81 (0)3 3409 1909
coffeehousenishiya.com

④
Switch Coffee Tokyo, Meguro
Backstreet local

Masahiro Onishi learnt how to roast coffee beans during stints in Melbourne and Fukuoka before opening the highly acclaimed Switch Coffee in Meguro in 2013.
1-17-23 Meguro, Meguro-ku
+81 (0)3 6420 3633
switchcoffeetokyo.com

⑤
Allpress, Kiyosumi
Kiwi connection

Michael Allpress started serving espressos from a cart in Auckland in the mid-1980s. Fast forward three decades and his company, Allpress Espresso, has opened this roastery in Tokyo, which also happens to be its first in Japan.

The building, designed by Japanese architect Taiichiro Suzuki to resemble the lumberyard shed that it replaced, also has a café that doubles as a training centre for new baristas. Go for the flat whites and western-style breakfast, including egg, avocado and tomato on toast, and granola.
3-7-2 Hirano, Koto-ku
+81 (0)3 5875 9392
jp.allpressespresso.com/en

Fuglen, Tomigaya
Nordic influence

Fuglen – opened by Einar Kleppe
Holthe, Peppe Trulsen and Halvor
Skiftun Digernes – feels more like a
well-loved lounge than a café. It is
furnished with the best of 1950s
and 1960s Norwegian design; by
day it serves aromatic coffees and
at night it's an inviting bar.
1-16-11 Tomigaya, Shibuya-ku
+81 (0)3 3481 0884
fuglen.no

More
coffee!
This is a
thorough
review of
your café

6
Paddlers Coffee, Nishihara
Warm welcome

Two years after opening his first
coffee stand, Daisuke Matsushima
(pictured, on right) has moved into a
more permanent home in Nishihara.
It is here that the self-taught barista
whips up his espressos using beans
from Stumptown Coffee Roasters
in Portland, Oregon.
　The café has a lived-in feel to
it; Matsushima renovated the
40-year-old apartment space and
filled it with antique furniture,
vintage floorboards and old music
equipment, including vinyl and a
cassette player. On warm days the
coveted seats are put out front in
the shade of a cherry-blossom tree.
2-26-5 Nishihara, Shibuya-ku
paddlerscoffee.com

⑧
The Monocle Café, Yurakucho
Coffee and Katsu-sando

At our café in Hankyu Men's department store you can read the latest issue while enjoying a cappuccino, a taco rice or *katsu sando* (pork-cutlet sandwich). We have made sure the furniture feels right too, with Bolichwerke lampshades and chairs by Maruni Wood Industry.
B1F, Hankyu Men's,
2-5-1 Yurakucho, Chiyoda-ku
+81 (0)3 6252 5285

Sweet treats

Japanese love a wedge of chiffon cake or baumkuchen. Try these three places for a refined sugar hit: Haritts (*haritts.com*); home-baked cake shop Merci Bake (*mercibake.com*); or first-rate patisserie Sadaharu Aoki (*sadaharuaoki.com*).

Tea
True brews

①

Sakurai Japanese Tea Experience, Nishi Azabu
Twist on tradition

A cup of green tea at Shinya Sakurai's exquisite modern tearoom is a serene experience. Customers sit at a counter while Sakurai offers them a selection of the finest teas in Japan, along with his own blends or teas with added herbs and fruits. Water is poured from an iron kettle using a wooden ladle.

Order some fresh Japanese *wagashi* sweets or even a glass of saké. Sakurai has a shop at the front selling teas, tools of the trade and takeaway drinks for those in a hurry.
3-16-28 Nishi Azabu, Minato-ku
+81 (0)3 5786 0024
sakurai-tea.jp

②
Ippodo, Marunouchi
Matcha made in heaven

For green-tea novices who don't know their *matcha* from their *gyokuro*, an afternoon at this bustling Kaboku tearoom is the ideal introduction. The tearoom on Naka-Dori near Yurakucho is run by Ippodo, a Kyoto company that has been selling green tea since 1717.

Japanese tea can be a complicated business but Kaboku offers top-quality drinks in a relaxed environment. *Matcha*, a thick whisked tea, is the most traditional of the lot and is usually for tea ceremonies; *sencha* is an everyday tea that is drunk hot or cold; and *genmaicha* combines green tea with toasted rice. The waitresses are happy to take charge but those who prefer to prepare their own are given the leaves, cups, hot water and even a clock for precision steeping, all served on a tray with seasonal Kyoto confectionery.
3-1-1 Marunouchi, Chiyoda-ku
+81 (0)3 6212 0202
ippodo-tea.co.jp/en

Saké
Rice-wine standouts

Bars
After-dark favourites

①

Akaoni, Sangenjaya
Top selection

Japanese have been brewing saké from fermented rice, *koji* yeast and water for more than two millennia. Also known as *nihon-shu*, the drink is marginally higher in alcohol content than wine. At Akaoni, a 38-seat *izakaya* in Sangenjaya, you will find an excellent selection from Japan's 1,500 breweries.

Opened in 1982 by Satoru Takizawa, this restaurant has 80 types of premium saké and a fish menu that changes daily. There's no English menu but the friendly staff will guide you with recommendations for food-and-drink pairings.
2-15-3 Sangenjaya, Setagaya-ku
+81 (0)3 3410 9918
akaoni39.com

②
Zorome, Monzen-Nakacho
Saké and small bites

Hisato Ono knew what kind of saké bar he wanted to become a regular at – and so opened it himself. Zorome has just eight seats at a long wooden counter and the place fills up soon after it opens at 18.00. There is no English sign so look for a white doorway with 1.8ltr bottles lined up outside.

Saké can of course be enjoyed on its own but it is often better when paired with food. To draw out the drink's hidden flavours, Ono prepares a range of tapas-sized dishes, including *chawan-mushi* made with egg and *dashi* broth, and sashimi.
1-12-6 Tomioka, Koto-ku
+81 (0)3 5875 8382

③
Sakeria SakeBozu, Tomigaya
Added complexity

Hidden away on the second floor of an old grey-tiled apartment building is SakeBozu, the small saké bar run by Tomo Maeda. Maeda mainly serves *junmai-shu* from tiny breweries that specialise in saké with robust, complex flavours.
Ronner YS Building 201,
1-37-1 Tomigaya, Shibuya-ku
+81 (0)3 3466 1311
sakebozu.com

①
Wine Shop & Diner Fujimaru, Asakusabashi
Global gathering

Opened in 2014 on the city's east side, this is the Tokyo branch of Osaka-based Wine Shop Fujimaru. With its stash of 1,500 bottles from the world's finest regions, Fujimaru caters to restaurateurs and wine aficionados as well as having a 19-seat diner.

Owner Tomofumi Fujimaru's idea was to feature affordable table wines, including those produced from Japanese grapes at his own Shimanouchi Fujimaru Winery in Osaka.
2F, S Building, 2-27-19 Higashi Nihonbashi, Chuo-ku
+81 (0)3 5829 8190
papilles.net

②
Trench, Ebisu
In the mix

Takuya Itoh's import business Small Axe aims to introduce handmade spirits and liqueurs to Japanese bartenders. The company also runs two bars and a coffee shop. Rogerio Igarashi Vaz is the barman in charge at Bar Trench, a book-lined establishment in Ebisu.

It is small enough that it is best to book ahead but once inside you'll want to work through the inviting menu. The Monkey Gin Fizz – with egg white and mandarin bitters – is bubbly and creamy. Warning: the absinthe cocktails are lethal.
1-5-8 Ebisu Nishi, Shibuya-ku
+81 (0)3 3780 5291
small-axe.net/bar-trench

These absinthe cocktails are just delishush

Y&M Bar Kisling, Ginza
Authentic take

Tokyo's Ginza district is where you'll find Japan's top bartenders plying their trade, honing their skills and upholding a tradition at what the Japanese call "authentic bars". Amid the area's neon signs and hidden lounges, discerning drinkers head to Seiichi Serizawa's Y&M Kisling.

Owner Serizawa has assembled an experienced team that includes veterans Takao Mori and Nobuo Abe. The ambience is a classic Japanese interpretation of an old-world bar, with white-jacketed waiters and impeccable service.
7F, 7-5-4 Ginza, Chuo-ku
+81 (0)3 3573 2071
homepage3.nifty.com/barkisling

④
Old Imperial Bar, Hibiya
Former glories

As the name suggests, the Imperial Hotel is a thoroughly classy establishment and has been in business since 1890. The Old Imperial Bar on the second-floor mezzanine exhibits the best traits of an old-school approach.

Sit at the long counter and sip cocktails made meticulously by bartenders in bow ties. And note the Oya stone and terracotta walls: they are from the 1923 building designed by Frank Lloyd Wright that was demolished to make way for the current digs, which date back to 1968.
1-1-1 Uchisaiwaicho, Chiyoda-ku
+81 (0)3 3539 8088
imperialhotel.co.jp

Retail
—— Shop talk

Nowhere else on the planet can match Tokyo for shopping. When it comes to customer service, choice and sheer quality, the city is without parallel.

Whether you're shopping in a giant department store, a traditional sweet shop or a cult fashion boutique, staff will be polite and attentive. Once you make a purchase the goods are beautifully wrapped and handed over with care. Japanese shoppers expect the best and retailers don't like to disappoint. Buyers leave no stone unturned in hunting out the latest products from Japan and beyond; the selection is never less than dazzling.

Tokyo is overflowing with fresh retail concepts and every sector of the market is catered for; men have two department stores all to themselves. You might not plan for it but a visit to this city will always involve some serious shopping; resistance is futile.

Clothing shops
Best dressed

45rpm, Aoyama
Committed to craft

Japanese fashion label 45rpm started out as a small operation about 40 years ago. It now has dozens of shops across Japan and a handful overseas. The brand is best known for its indigo cottons and denims but the full collection runs from T-shirts to overcoats.

The design team is relentless in its pursuit of original fabrics whether collaborating with weavers in northern Japan or remote mills in the Shetlands. A tranquil wooden house behind a leafy gate, the Minami Aoyama flagship showcases this commitment to craftsmanship.
7-7-21 Minami Aoyama, Minato-ku
+81 (0)3 5778 0045
45rpm.jp

③ Mackintosh, Aoyama
Rain check

In 2007, Japanese trading company Yagi Tsusho bought Mackintosh, reviving this famed Scottish manufacturer of rubberised raincoats. Its beautiful Aoyama store (by retail-design maestro Masamichi Katayama) showcases how far the brand has come.

While still referencing its heritage as the original rainwear, the silhouettes are sharper. Washed wool duffles, weather-proof parkas and collaborations with the likes of Tokyo brand Hyke make this an essential stop for anyone in the market for outerwear.
5-3-20 Minami Aoyama, Minato-ku
+81 (0)3 6418 5711
mackintosh.com/jp

② En Route, Ginza
Winning style

Sport and fashion collide at En Route, a new addition to the United Arrows stable (*see page 48*). At the label's shop and running station in Ginza, one floor is devoted to workout clothes. The other houses urban fashion: a fresh, wearable selection that mixes En Route's own label with Japanese brands such as Teatora and Comoli. Fitness gear includes shoes by Nike and technical wear by Descente. Staff also post weather reports and running routes while Schemata Architects' Jo Nagasaka has given the space an airy industrial flavour.
3-10-6 Ginza, Chuo-ku
+81 (0)3 3541 9020
enroute.tokyo

I think a large coat is in order

④ Classico, Yanaka
Local hero

At his shop Classico, Ryu Takahashi sells antiques, clothes (for men and women) and crafts. But his speciality is promoting small brands that share his belief in making products locally. Much of his stock is made in Japan: A Vontade jackets, shirts from Nisica and Yaeca, Shoes Like Pottery trainers and ceramics made in Okinawa kilns.

The shop, which opened in Yanaka in 2006, also sells its own line of Oxford shirts that Takahashi orders from a small Tokyo factory. For a two-room shop it's an impressive and diverse collection; quality and provenance are more important to Takahashi than fashion. He also has a knack for finding well-designed items that you will want to hold on to for some time to come.
2-5-22 Yanaka, Taito-ku
+81 (0)3 3823 7622
classico-life.com

I relax in my 'yukata' after a hard day of rest

Built for comfort — Motoji's 'yukatas' are custom-made

⑤ 1LDK, Nakameguro
Branded together

Tokyo has made an art of the select shop where brands are grouped together and repackaged. One example is 1LDK, which sells a mix of labels, including Tokyo brand Digawel and its own line Universal Products.

Located in Nakameguro (which offers pleasant riverside strolls), the main menswear shop is on one side of the street with more across the road, as well as womenswear and accessories. Other members of the 1LDK family include the Taste and Sense restaurant and 1LDK Aoyama Hotel.
1-8-28 Kamimeguro, Meguro-ku
+81 (0)3 3780 1645
1ldkshop.com

⑥ Ginza Motoji, Ginza
Robe trader

One of the pleasures of a night in a Japanese inn is the cotton *yukata* robe provided for your stay. If you want your own, consider a custom-made one from Motoji, which has adjacent shops in Ginza for men and women. In producing the robes, company president Komei Motoji (*pictured, on left*) brims with ideas such as using Ginza's willow trees for dye.

Before stepping onto the *tatami* mat for a fitting, sift through the shop's selection of prints and weaves. The *yukata* will be shipped to your home in about four weeks.
3-8-15 Ginza, Chuo-ku
+81 (0)3 5524 7472
motoji.co.jp

7

Ts(s) and Toujours, Ebisu
Two's company

Takuji Suzuki, a former stylist and creative director, launched his fashion label Ts in 1999 and renamed it Ts(s) 10 years later. He also helped his wife Masayo Shimeno create her own brand, Toujours. The couple (*pictured*) now share staff and space – part studio, part shop – on a backstreet between Daikanyama and Ebisu, a preference for working with factories in Japan and a desire to create new items that can also be mixed and matched with their past collections.

This dedication to original combinations, as well as the fact that the Ts(s) and Toujours collections bear little similarity to one another, have won the couple deep admiration from their loyal clientele. Time your visit carefully, mind you: Ts(s) is only open on Fridays and Saturdays.
1F, 1-29-5 Ebisu Nishi, Shibuya-ku
+81 (0)3 5939 8090
notsohardwork.com

8

Tomorrowland, Shibuya
Quality mix

Hiroyuki Sasaki has been raising the bar for fashion in Japan since he founded his company in 1978. The Tomorrowland shops for men and women are top quality, mixing pieces from the company's own labels with inspired accessories by other brands.

Tomorrowland has its own sub-labels with their own shops, including Galerie Vie and Des Prés (both for women). The company has also brought standalone shops to Japan by the likes of Acne Studios, Isabel Marant, Umit Benan and Dries Van Noten.
1-23-16 Shibuya, Shibuya-ku
+81 (0)3 5774 1711
tomorrowland.co.jp

9

Galerie Vie, Marunouchi
Relaxed focus

Galerie Vie has been selling its women's clothes since 1985. Part of the Tomorrowland group, the label keeps its focus clear and simple with relaxed clothes in quality natural fabrics. The basic palette centres on white, grey, navy and black with seasonal colour bursts.

Knitwear is a particular strength: cotton for summer, cashmere for winter and hand-knits for both. There are subtle changes between the seasons, with bigger volume pieces such as mohair sweaters for winter.
2F, Shin Marunouchi Building,
1-5-1 Marunouchi, Chiyoda-ku
+81 (0)3 5224 8677
galerievie.jp

10

FilMelange, Gaienmae
Original cut

Using threads specially developed for the label, FilMelange has been making top-quality sweatshirts, hoodies, T-shirts, underwear and track pants since 2007. The stock comes in a range of colours and is sized for men, women and kids. Extras include socks and jeans.
1F, 2-6-6 Jingumae, Shibuya-ku
+81 (0)3 6447 1107
filmelange.com

⑪
United Arrows, Harajuku
Young and old

Thanks to co-founders Yasuto
Kamoshita and Hirofumi Kurino
United Arrows has, over the course
of a quarter of a century, become a
hugely powerful force in the world
of fashion.

With more than a dozen
sub-brands, including the elegant
Drawer label for women, United
Arrows has a broad audience. Its
new generation of taste-makers is
led by Motofumi "Poggy" Kogi,
director of United Arrows & Sons.
This young brand, which occupies
the ground and basement levels
of the men's flagship store in
Harajuku, reflects Poggy's eclectic
style: a mix of street fashion and
classic tailoring. The shop also
boasts the pick of the newest
international fashion brands. There
is a café for a coffee or cocktail
and upstairs you will find tailoring,
shirts and shoes.
3-28-1 Jingumae, Shibuya-ku
+81 (0)3 3479 8180
united-arrows.jp

Perfect picks
---
01 Cotton suit by Nigold
02 Indigo-dyed sweatshirt by
United Arrows & Sons
03 Hat by Takayuki Kijima
04 Casual suit by The
Stylist Japan
05 Chino trousers by Kolor

The door was bigger on the way in

Winning combo
—
Arts & Science offers fashion and homeware

⑫
Beams, Harajuku
Street life

Beams started as a small fashion boutique in Harajuku back in 1976. Today it is one of Japan's biggest retailers with shops all over the country that appeal to different audiences.

This corner of Harajuku is Beams central with shops including Beams F for classic wear and Beams T for limited-edition T-shirts. Beams International Gallery has the pick of the world's top fashion names – including Japanese labels such as Sacai – plus *mingei* (folk) Japanese homeware in the Fennica section.
3-24-7 Jingumae, Shibuya-ku
+81 (0)3 3470 3947
beams.co.jp

⑬
Over The Counter, Aoyama
Service with a smile

Tokyo-based stylist-turned-retailer Sonya Park (*pictured*) has carved her own niche with Arts & Science, the brand she started in 2003. She has eight outlets in the city, including a café and gallery space. On offer is a creative mix of clothes for men and women plus accessories and homeware. Over the Counter – one of several Arts & Science shops in the neighbourhood – sells cutlery, soap, ceramics and stationery from home and abroad, plus original leather goods.
101 Palace Miyuki, 5-3-8 Minami Aoyama, Minato-ku
+81 (0)3 3400 1009
arts-science.com

14
Loopwheeler, Sendagaya
Industrial revolution

Developed for university playing fields and marketed to urbanites, sweatshirts have been a quintessential piece of casualwear for more than a century. Satoshi Suzuki (*pictured*), founder of Loopwheeler, has shown that in the right hands a sweatshirt can also be a highly coveted fashion item. What differentiates his sweatshirts is the antiquated contraption he uses in their production: a loophole circular knitting machine.

A relic from early 20th-century manufacturing, loopwheel machines were rendered almost obsolete by the shift to low-cost plants in other parts of Asia. However, Suzuki launched his casualwear brand in 1999 with the aim of saving what remained of these machines at factories in Wakayama.

Each loopwheel machine produces just one metre of cloth an hour – or enough for eight sweatshirts a day. From this Suzuki produces every sweatshirt, cardigan and T-shirt that his team designs and sells at two shops in Sendagaya: the main outlet and a second space upstairs, Loopwheeler Vintage Service, which stocks pieces from past collections. With his focus on quality and craftsmanship, Suzuki's brand has earned a keen following. He has also collaborated with the likes of Nike, Margaret Howell and Japanese select shop Beams.
*B1F/2F, Yamana Building,
3-51-3 Sendagaya, Shibuya-ku
+81 (0)3 5414 2350
loopwheeler.co.jp*

Factory fashion
—
The focus is on craft and quality

Perfect picks
—
01 Light high-neck hoodie
02 Kanoko button-down polo
03 Basic crewneck set-in sleeve pullover
04 Light hoodie for women
05 Inlaid shorts

⑮ Engineered Garments, Aoyama
Dedicated approach

New York-based Japanese designer Daiki Suzuki's clothes are available around the city but this is the brand's own shop. The outlet sells the label's men's and womenswear, including khaki cotton twill trousers, blue chambray shirts and seersucker jackets.
*5-11-15 Minami Aoyama, Minato-ku
+81 (0)3 6419 1798
nepenthes.co.jp*

⑯ FIL, Omotesando
Quality counts

Today Hiroki Nakamura's brand enjoys cult status but that doesn't mean he has lost sight of the passionate attention to detail that has been key to his label since it was founded in 2000. His Social Sculpture Denim is a case in point. Although inspired by American vintage it remains pure Visvim: from the yarn to the indigo-dyed deerskin patch, everything is made especially for Nakamura and the denim, which gets better with age, is woven on selvedge looms.

The basement FIL Tokyo store carries all the favourites, including the much-loved FBT shoes that combine a suede upper with a trainer sole. The nearby Visvim store in the Gyre building has exclusive items, women's line WMV and a café: Little Cloud Coffee.
*Visvim: 2F, Gyre, 5-10-1 Jingumae, Shibuya-ku; +81 (0)3 5468 5424
FIL Tokyo: B1F, 5-9-17 Jingumae, Shibuya-ku; +81 (0)3 5725 9568
visvim.tv*

⑰ Anatomica, Higashi Nihonbashi
Paris-Tokyo express

Pierre Fournier, who started fashion retailer Anatomica in Paris in 1994, chose Tokyo for the location of his second standalone store. The shop occupies a street-level plot in a neighbourhood facing the Kanda River in Higashi Nihonbashi, far from the city's most fashionable districts.

It marks Fournier's second foray into Tokyo, following his shop-in-shop at United Arrows. Fournier and business partner Kinji Teramoto wanted a space off the main street and they have mainly filled it with men's clothing of their own designs. Fournier and Teramoto's collaborations include "Made in Japan" jeans and Shetland-wool sweaters. Luis Ameztoy conceived the plywood-and-metal design.
*S Building, 2-27-19 Higashi Nihonbashi, Chuo-ku
+81 (0)3 5823 6186
anatomica.jp*

My career as an expert wrapper is showing great promise

Department stores
All under one roof

Tokyo's many department stores prove that there is still life in this traditional retail format. These giant emporia have had to rethink their strategy in recent years to keep up with the times and they go out of their way to appeal to customers with seasonal displays and the newest labels. They are also known for excellent kitchenware departments and the basement food halls – *depachika* – are the best in the world. Don't forget to visit the rooftop, where you are likely to find some open space and a small shrine.

01 Isetan, Shinjuku
Isetan Shinjuku is the most dynamic of the department stores and is the leading outlet for fashion; the women's shoe department on the second floor is as vast as the jeans bar is comprehensive. They also carry every new label you've only just heard of and host pop-ups for Japanese brands. Male customers have their own building with nine floors of fashion, plus a rooftop golf school.
isetan.mistore.jp/store/shinjuku

02 Matsuya, Ginza
Head to the seventh floor of this Ginza department store for the Design Collection, a selection of items chosen by the great and good of the Japanese design world. It is perfect for Japanese homeware, whether a stool by Isamu Kenmochi or *washi* paper lights. Matsuya is one of three historic department stores in Ginza: Mitsukoshi can be found a few doors along, while neighbouring Matsuzakaya was closed in 2013 but is set to be reborn as a luxury retail development in 2017.
matsuya.com/m_ginza

03 Mitsukoshi, Ginza
This is the grande dame of Tokyo department stores: Mitsukoshi boasts a history stretching back to 1673. The old-school Nishonbashi store even has its own metro station: Mitsukoshimae. The Ginza branch, a landmark at the corner of Ginza crossing, reopened after a major refurbishment in 2010 and now has a smart new annexe.
mitsukoshi.mistore.jp/store/ginza

(18)
Nook Store, Daikanyama
World of its own

Women's fashion in Japan very much follows its own path, which makes shopping a scintillating business for anyone from overseas. Nook Store in Daikanyama fuses clothes and lifestyle in an artfully underdressed shop. Earthy tableware and bottles of organic juice sit on the shelves alongside Catworth dance shoes and loose cotton sweaters. As well as its Nook and Cranny brand there are pieces from young Japanese brands such as Comoli and Auralee. It's a carefully thought-out world.
14-12 Sarugaku-cho, Shibuya-ku
+81 (0)3 6416 1044
nookstore.jp

Perfect picks
—
01 Jeans by Nook and Cranny
02 White Series enamel containers by Noda Horo
03 Napkins by R&D.M.Co
04 Leather shoes by Shoe & Sewn
05 Cotton shirt by Auralee

19
Goro, Honkomagome
Made to last

People come from all over Japan
to buy walking boots from Goro.
Owner Isao Morimoto is the son
of a Tokyo shoemaker and grew up
making boots; he has been working
on his off-road shoes since 1973.

Fans come from all walks of
life, be they students or hikers. The
boots are cut by hand and made in
Morimoto's small Tokyo workshop.
He draws an outline of each
customer's foot so that the team
(*pictured*) can get the fit just right;
a good all-round boot is the light
but durable Bootie-L. Meanwhile,
Morimoto has worked with a wax-
maker in Nishi Nippori in Tokyo
to develop the perfect wax.

Look after them and these boots
will be good for years but if you
need repairs you can send them
back. It's in an obscure location but
head next door to Grand Route 66
for exceptionally good curry rice.
6-4-2 Honkomagome, Bunkyo-ku
+81 (0)3 3945 0855
goro.co.jp

*I've run out
of shoe wax!
I must get
to Goro at
once!*

Outdoor wear

Seventy per cent of Japan's terrain is mountainous so it's natural that the country excels at outdoor gear. Here are five brands that make everything from jackets to tents.

01 The North Face Standard, Harajuku: It's a brand that is usually worn by rock climbers and alpinists. The North Face Standard shop, opened in 2010, also targets another crowd: fashionable urbanites. The trench coats, shirts and booties are designed in Japan by sportswear retail and marketing company Goldwin.
goldwin.co.jp/tnf

02 Snow Peak, Marunouchi: Camping-gear brand Snow Peak's shop next to Tokyo Station sells a selection of the Niigata-based company's catalogue, including its waterproof tents, cast-iron cookware and super-light titanium cups and cutlery.
snowpeak.co.jp

03 And Wander, citywide: Founded in 2011 by Mihoko Mori and Keita Ikeuchi (both formerly with fashion label Issey Miyake), And Wander makes jackets, fleeces, base layers and backpacks.
andwander.com

04 Descente, Harajuku: This outfitter for Japan's Winter Olympics opened its flagship store in 2013 offering sportswear and casuals, including the Allterrain collection that uses only high-performance textiles.
descente.jp

05 MontBell, Shibuya: This five-storey emporium stocks tents, sleeping bags and jackets alongside essentials for fishing, climbing and cycling.
en.montbell.jp

Home and interiors
Design for living

 ①
Yaeca Home Store, Shirokane
Fashion to live by

Twelve years after they started Yaeca, their fashion brand, Tetsuhiro Hattori and Kyoko Ide decided to showcase their clothes in a home setting. They rented a 40-year-old house in the residential Shirokane area and stripped back the interior to create the stunning Yaeca Home Store.

Here they sell their men's and womenswear alongside a selection of vintage furniture, plates and jewellery that dates from the 1930s to 1970s. The clothes are made in Japan, mostly in Tohoku, and the range includes denim, knits and a line called Stock, which uses organic thread.

To complete the home feeling there is an open-brick fireplace and a pantry corner for new brand Plain Bakery, selling eggs, biscuits and granola. You might want to move in.
4-7-10 Shirokane, Minato-ku
+81 (0)3 6277 1371
yaeca.com/home

②
Imabari Towel Shop, Aoyama
Dryer's delight

The city of Imabari in Ehime prefecture means one thing: towels. When cheap imports threatened to destroy the Japanese towel industry, local makers fought back with a new shared mark of quality by top designer Kashiwa Sato. The Imabari Towel Shop in Aoyama showcases the best from the city's manufacturers (there are 116 in the Shikoku Towel Industrial

Association) and its staff will help you find the right pile, weave and waffle from a wide selection.
2F, From-First Building, 5-3-10 Minami Aoyama, Minato-ku
+81 (0)3 6427 2941
imabaritoweljapan.jp

③
D47, Shibuya
Everyday quality

Kenmei Nagaoka's main business was in graphic design but an interest in vintage furniture led him to open D&Department, a shop focused on secondhand pieces and Japanese goods still in production but overlooked. D&Department now has branches all over Japan, supporting Nagaoka's ongoing mission against homogenisation. At the D47 shop in Hikarie in Shibuya you'll find crafts and food products from around Japan. There's also an exhibition space and a restaurant serving regional food.
8F, Hikarie, 2-21-1 Shibuya, Shibuya-ku
+81 (0)3 6427 2302
hikarie8.com/d47designtravelstore

④
Cibone, Gaienmae
Made in Japan

Since opening in 2001, interiors shop Cibone has been a beacon for imaginative retailing courtesy of Masaki Yokokawa (*pictured*). The shop's move to its new location in 2014 marked a greater emphasis on products made in Japan. Alongside, say, a Workstead floor light from Brooklyn or a dresser from Danish company Gubi, you are likely to find wooden boxes handmade in Matsumoto. Vintage and one-off pieces now mix with kitchenware, Japanese ceramics and clothes from labels such as Taro Horiuchi.
2F, 2-27-25 Minami Aoyama, Minato-ku
+81 (0)3 3475 8017
cibone.com

⑤
Bingoya, Wakamatsu-cho
Countrywide craft

Anyone interested in Japanese *mingei* (folk art) should make their way to Bingoya, a delightfully old-fashioned craft shop spread over five floors. It stocks regional crafts objects from all over Japan: Okinawan ceramics, paper boxes from Toyama and cherry-bark tea caddies from Akita. Other items include indigo *jinbei* pyjamas, lacquer rice bowls, glassware and *kokeshi* dolls. Bags of atmosphere and a good stop for anyone who isn't heading into the countryside. Open since the early 1960s, this is a Tokyo gem.
10-6 Wakamatsu-cho, Shinjuku-ku
+81 (0)3 3202 8778
quasar.nu/bingoya

Kama Asa Shoten, Kappabashi
The professionals' choice

Kama Asa Shoten is located in Kappabashi, where the city's restaurateurs go to stock up on kitchen supplies. The shop attracts chefs for its high-quality tools of the trade: more than 1,000 knives along with cast-iron pans, hand-pounded aluminium pots, wasabi graters, *yakitori* grills and many other essentials.

Founded in 1908, the shop occupies two buildings separated by an alleyway and it's still a family enterprise, now headed by fourth-generation scion Daisuke Kumazawa.
2-24-1 Matsugaya, Taito-ku
+81 (0)3 3841 9355
kama-asa.co.jp

⑦
Tokyo Hands, Shibuya
A shop for everyone

If you visit just one shop during your stay here, make sure it is Tokyu Hands. It's a Tokyo institution that sells thousands of products for home and travel, from light bulbs to planks of wood. There are numerous branches but the heart and soul is the original shop in Shibuya. The store attracts more than five million visitors a year and among its roughly 150,000 items of merchandise are 14,000 pens and 18,000 kitchen goods.

There are more than 270 members of staff kitted out in green aprons and white shirts, their pockets loaded with notebooks and tape measures. Tokyu Hands is an egalitarian space: a shop for young and old, specialists and dilettantes, locals and tourists. Here you will find builders looking for tools mixing with young design students searching for creative materials.
12-18 Udagawa-cho, Shibuya-ku
+81 (0)3 5489 5111
shibuya.tokyu-hands.co.jp

Under the sun
—
Tokyu Hands attracts millions of visitors

 Hakusan Shop, Aoyama
Impeccable taste

Hakusan Toki has been making ceramics in Hasami on the island of Kyushu (one of Japan's pottery hotspots) since 1958 and many of the original designs are still in production. Masahiro Mori, the firm's late creative director, was a tabletop genius and his G-type soy sauce bottle is a classic that turns up in homes and restaurants all over Japan. More recent additions to the Hakusan product line include a series of rice bowls that come in an array of colours and patterns.
*B1F, From-First Building,
5-3-10 Minami Aoyama, Minato-ku
+81 (0)3 5774 8850
hakusan-shop.com*

⑨
Spiral Market, Aoyama
The perfect mix

So-called *zakka* shops, filled with miscellaneous goods, proliferate in Tokyo. But this example in the Spiral Building in Aoyama (designed by Fumihiko Maki, no less) is still one of the best: a comfortable mix of homeware, stationery, greetings cards and accessories from home and abroad. Here you can find good Japanese ceramics, glass from Tokyo maker Sugihara and cotton *tenugui* cloths. It is also home to Spiral Records, a longstanding source of good sounds old and new.
*2F, Spiral Building, 5-6-23
Minami Aoyama, Minato-ku
+81 (0)3 3498 5792
spiral.co.jp*

Perfect picks
—
01 Work Hands ×
Beams apron
02 Cypress bath stool
03 Wasabi grater
04 Japan-made nail clippers
05 Delfonics photo album

⑩
Maruni, Higashi Nihonbashi
Breakthrough design

Maruni's fortunes began to soar in 2005 when the firm started appearing at design fairs with chairs by high-profile designers. With Naoto Fukasawa as its creative director, The firm displays its chairs, tables and sofas in a gallery-like showroom space.
*3-6-13 Higashi Nihonbashi, Chuo-ku
+81 (0)3 3667 4021
maruni.com*

⑪
SyuRo, Kuramae
Bold and brassy

Designer Masuko Unayama
(*pictured, on right*), who started
her lifestyle brand SyuRo in 2000,
works with the city's forgotten
artisans to create her fine line
of household items. Opened in
2008, her shop stocks containers
made from tin, copper and
brass pounded into cylinders
and boxes by metalworkers who
have laboured in the city's small
backstreet factories for decades.

Their craft was all but dying out
until she helped bring attention to
what they do. The items she sells
are designed to be held on to for
generations; they gradually change
colour as they age and the metal
oxidises, giving them a patina of
imperfection that evokes their
handmade origins. Unayama has
also designed bags and pouches
made of repurposed tents and
fireproof sheets.
1-15-7 Torigoe, Taito-ku
+81 (0)3 3861 0675
syuro.info

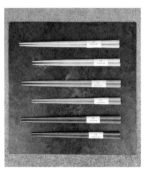

Accessories and specialist retailers
Bits and bobs

①
Continuer, Ebisu
Frame up

When he opened his eyewear shop
in Tokyo's Ebisu district more than
a decade ago, Shuji Shimazaki
envisioned a salon for designers
and artists. Nowadays his staff
explain the details of frames from
more than two dozen brands.

To amass the collection,
Shimazaki goes on scouting trips
with employees to international
exhibitions and tiny workshops in
remote parts of Japan. One key
find: acetate frames crafted by Jun
Tsuchiya, who makes only a few
dozen of them a month under his
brand 12 Home Made.
2-9-2 Ebisu Minami, Shibuya-ku
+81 (0)3 3792 8978
continuer.jp

②
Shed That Roared, Meguro
Passion for leather

When cabinet maker Ken Nishijo
worked on an interior for a Tokyo
leather-bag maker in 2001, he
asked the company to make him a
tool bag. Nishijo loved it so much
that he started a side business in
them: Raregem makes leather
shoulder bags, created by that same
manufacturer, and robust totes from
a tough Kurashiki-made canvas.
Other products include brass hooks,
wooden hanging pegs and canvas
aprons. Meguro shop Shed That
Roared showcases the products –
and the team's interior-design skills.
Open Thursday to Saturday.
1-1-11 Ohashi, Meguro-ku
+81 (0)3 6427 8485
raregem.co.jp

③
Postalco, Shibuya
Duly noted

The main shop for Tokyo
stationery brand Postalco has
a retro feel; think *Mad Men* in
Shibuya. The company started
almost by accident when founder
Mike Abelson made an A4
envelope case with a button
fastener for his wife Yuri.

The Tokyo shop sells notebooks,
wallets, bags and the original
envelope holders in different sizes.
There are also collaboration items
– including one with MONOCLE –
and useful Totem brass keyrings
made individually in Japan.
3F, Yamaji Building,
1-6-3 Dogenzaka, Shibuya-ku
+81 (0)3 6455 0531
postalco.net

Playing shop
—
Kodomo Beams is best for kids

Kids' clothes are a good fit for me, OK?

④
Kodomo Beams, Daikanyama
Child's play

Children might be happy with anything pink and plastic but their parents will thank you for dropping in on Kodomo Beams, one of the best kids' shops in Tokyo. The work of fashion retailer Beams (*see page 49*), this shop in Daikanyama has a terrific selection of its own brand of mini clothes and a pick of others, including Patagonia and New Balance.

There are wooden blocks from Japanese textile label Minä Perhonen and multicoloured rucksacks. Furniture includes a desk by Beams and Landscape Products and a Plankton chair from Graf in Osaka. This place has all the basics that every Japanese child needs, including indoor shoes and raincoats, plus baby essentials and a Japan-made heat-resistant baby tableware line called Iiwan.
19-7 Sarugaku-cho, Shibuay-ku
+81 (0)3 5428 4844
beams.co.jp/labels/detail/
kodomo-beams

⑤
Lisn, Aoyama
Heaven scent

If incense brings to mind a fug of patchouli then the light, clean smells of Lisn should change your mind. The Kyoto incense-maker has a beautifully simple shop in Aoyama (above APC) selling the brand's short incense sticks.

Each fragrance has been given a poetic name such as Mountain, Sea Foam or Largo. Customers can sniff their way through the selection and the sticks are packed in neat tubes or sachets. There are limited-edition seasonal fragrances and a good selection of holders.
202, 5-47-13 Jingumae, Shibuya-ku
+81 (0)3 5469 5006
lisn.co.jp/aoyama

⑥
Fuga, Gaienmae
Bouquets all round

Florist Miyuki Kobayashi keeps on top of trends by going to Tokyo's biggest flower market three times a week at 06.00. She can do arrangements of any size and in any style. Known for its fresh blooms, the shop is always ablaze with colour.
1F/BF1, Aoyama MS Building,
3-7-5 Jingumae, Shibuya-ku
+81 (0)3 5410 3707
fuga-tokyo.com/jp

MONOCLE

NEW YORK TORONTO LONDON ZÜRICH   ISTANBUL SINGAPORE HONG KONG TOKYO

Tokyo edition
Come and say hello to our editorial team

⑦

The Monocle Shop, Tomigaya
Limited edition

This is where you will find every issue of the magazine dating back to the beginning (March 2007), our annual look-ahead publication THE FORECAST and summer special THE ESCAPIST. The shelves are stocked with products that we have developed in collaboration with our favourite brands from around the world. Pick from Rimowa luggage, Porter bags, Revo radios, Caran d'Ache pens and our own Voyage travel collection.

Occupying a space behind the shop is our editorial and sales team. If you're in the area, stop by, say hello and pick up our map, which has recommendations for places in the neighbourhood to eat, drink and shop. From here it's a short subway ride to the Monocle Café (*see page 41*) in the Hankyu Men's Building in Yurakucho.
1F, Luna Rossa, 1-19-2 Tomigaya, Shibuya-ku
+81 (0)3 6407 0845
monocle.com

Perfect picks
—
01 'The Monocle Guide to Good Business'
02 Monocle × Rimowa Multiwheel suitcase
03 Revo Monocle 24 SuperConnect radio
04 Monocle accordion pocket notebook
05 Monocle Voyage travel jacket

⑧

Takeo Paper Shop, Kanda
Wrappers' delight

Founded in 1899, Tokyo-based speciality-paper purveyor Takeo opened its flagship shop in 2000. Mainly a distributor, the family-run company also works with book, package and graphic designers and domestic paper mills to develop small-lot, high-quality paper.

The shop was designed by Sanaa's Ryue Nishizawa; swatches of paper sit on tables and drawers stuffed with A4-sized sheets are built into the walls. Its paper is used for lithographs, customised packing and art books.
3-18-3 Kanda Nishiki-cho, Chiyoda-ku
+81 (0)3 3292 3669
takeo.co.jp

⑨

Edoya, Nihonbashi
Brush with tradition

Edoya was awarded its title as a paintbrush-maker in 1718 by the Tokugawa Shogunate and remains one of Nihonbashi's most well-known institutions. It started making clothes brushes in the 19th century when western fashion came into vogue and today makes everything from hair brushes to toothbrushes.

Although the raw materials are increasingly difficult to source, Edoya still makes its products by hand, using pig bristle, horse and boar hair, with cherry wood and beech wood for the handles.
2-16 Nihonbashi Odenma-cho, Chuo-ku
+81 (0)3 3664 5671
nihonbashi-edoya.co.jp

Going beyond mere function

10
Hakui, Kappabashi
Uniform design

Akira Onozuka doesn't think of workwear as fashion. But having spent 13 years with Issey Miyake and more than two decades running his own label, Zucca, he makes uniforms for chefs, hotel staff and museum attendants that go beyond the mere functional.

In 1991 Onozuka started Hakui (White Coat) with Japanese manufacturer Seven Uniform, which recently renovated his showroom in Kappabashi to house the collection. Some of Onozuka's old designs – gingham shirts from two decades ago, for instance – still sell briskly.

Onozuka creates three-quarter-sleeve sweatshirts, sturdy jackets and *kappogi* (traditional cooking aprons) that could pass as casualwear but are made to be stain-resistant and wrinkle-free. His workwear collections are popular among young shopkeepers, café owners and boutique hotels.
hakui-shop.com

Concept stores
Mixed retail

①
Claska, Meguro
Old and new

What started out in 2008 as a gift and craft shop inside Meguro's Hotel Claska has now expanded to several branches. Under director Takeo Okuma, Claska offers a mix of traditional craft, everyday homeware and modern design. Goods include straw hats from Saitama and cutlery from Niigata; there are also items by craftspeople who Okuma has met on his trips around Japan.

Okuma firmly believes that traditional and new products can, with the right presentation, sit side by side. He has a point: against a Claska pale-wood interior, a classic flowery bowl from Kanazawa suddenly looks modern.
2F, Claska, 1-3-18 Chuo-cho, Meguro-ku
+81 (0)3 3719 8124
do.claska.com

Maach Ecute Kanda Manseibashi,
Kanda
Station to station

Brick-built Manseibashi Station,
next to hi-tech Akihabara, had stood
idle for 70 years before undergoing
renovation in a joint project by
Japan Rail East Retailing and
Yokohama architecture firm Mikan.
The transformation was stunning,
shaping the original features into
a new retail and exhibition space
called Maach Ecute.

Top retail picks include interiors
shop Haluta, patisserie Noake
Tokyo and wine shop Vinosity
Domi. Fukumori serves excellent
lunches with fresh ingredients from
Yamagata. The events schedule is
packed with exhibitions, live jazz
and pop-up shows. The architects
had the good sense to keep the
brickwork, arches and original
platform intact; sit in café N3331
and watch the trains going by.
*1-25-4 Kanda suda-cho, Chiyoda-ku
+81 (0)3 3257 8910
maach-ecute.jp*

**Maach Ecute
retailers**
—
01 Haluta (interior and fashion)
02 Obscura Coffee Roasters
03 N3331 café
04 Fukumori (café and
shop selling groceries from
Yamagata prefecture)
05 Hitachino Brewing Labo

③
Gekkoso, Ginza
Sound the horn

A quirky art-supplies shop on a
quiet street in Ginza, Gekkoso has
been in business since 1917. It sells
a broad selection of its own brand
of paints, brushes and pads of
paper. The shop logo – a post horn
– adorns a selection of cotton and
canvas bags, and there is a gallery
and small café downstairs. The
owners also run Tsuki no Hanare, a
café-bar nearby playing live music.
Gekkoso is close to the public bath
of Ginza Konparuyu, which is worth
a visit for a Japanese bath experience
and a taste of an older Tokyo.
*1F/B1F, Eiju Building, 8-7-2 Ginza,
Chuo-ku
+81 (0)3 3572 5605
gekkoso.jp*

④
Muji, Yurakucho
A brand apart

There are branches of Muji or
Mujirushi Ryohin (No Brand
Goods, to translate its full name)
all over Tokyo but the Yurakucho
mother ship has the full range,
from clothes and bicycles to a Muji
Café and even a Muji House show
home. The children's department
has a wooden play area for kids.
There's also a workshop for
alterations and an exhibition space.

Muji is a feature of Japanese life:
cheap and reliable. Crockery, made
in Japan, is a good deal; so too the
nylon holdalls for the inevitable
shopping overspill.
*3-8-3 Marunouchi, Chiyoda-ku
+81 (0)3 5208 8241
muji.net/shop*

⑤
La Kagu, Kagurazaka
Turning the page

A former book warehouse owned by Japanese publisher Shinchosha, La Kagu takes the lifestyle-shop concept in a new direction. Run by Sazaby League and designed by architect Kengo Kuma, the airy two-storey shop stocks menswear (including the company's own Hundredson label), womenswear, tools, kitchenware and vintage Danish furniture.

In the café, customers sit at long wooden tables enjoying gourmet hot dogs, charcuterie plates and cappuccinos. Unlike most select shops, La Kagu also sells books; hundreds of titles, not all published by Shinchosha, are kept upstairs where seats are set out for readings, lectures and music performances. La Kagu also hosts pop-up shops for small brands such as eyewear maker Ayame I Wear and fashion label Madisonblue.

67 Yarai-cho, Shinjuku-ku
+81 (0)3 5277 6977
lakagu.com

Print plethora
—
La Kagu stocks thousands of books

Bookshops
Good reads

①

Daikanyama T-Site, Daikanyama
Home entertainment

Tsutaya Books, at Daikanyama T-Site, is a bookshop with few equals. Designed by Tokyo-based architecture firm Klein Dytham, the shop consists of three two-storey buildings that opened in 2011. More than 140,000 books and magazines line the walls and sit on display tables; upstairs there are 80,000 DVDs and 100,000 CDs.

Don't miss the Anjin lounge, which has armchairs, art and a magazine archive, with waiters serving drinks and light meals. Also on the premises are a convenience store, café, restaurant, toy shop, dog-grooming and pet-hotel facility, electric-bicycle shop and speciality camera shop.
17-5 Sarugaku-cho, Shibuya-ku
+81 (0)3 3770 2525
real.tsite.jp/daikanyama/english/

Three more

01 Nostos Books, Setagaya: Specialises in second-hand books on design, art, photography and architecture, all selected by owner and designer Takashi Nakano.
nostos.jp

02 Shibuya Publishing & Booksellers, Shibuya: Open until midnight during the week, this bookshop offers a mix of magazines, manga, novels, photobooks and philosophy.
shibuyabooks.net

03 Aoyama Book Center, Aoyama: This bookshop features a staggering range of magazines from Japan and abroad, and is particularly strong on art, design and architecture.
aoyamabc.jp

Beams Records, Harajuku
Classic mix

If you've ever walked into a record shop and felt overwhelmed, tiny Beams Records will come as a well-honed relief. The music buyers here have done the hard work and brought together a compact selection of CDs and vinyl that, quite possibly, will be the new soundtrack to your life. Sounds range from hip-hop to folk and everything in between.

Extras include designer Koichi Futatsumata's beautifully minimal hybrid amplifier and a canvas bag for storing records from Tokyo brand Tembea. But don't stop there: there is plenty more to discover.
1F, 3-25-15 Jingumae, Shibuya-ku
+81 (0)3 3746 0789
beams.co.jp/shops/detail/
beams-records

Three more

01 Big Love, Sendagaya: Perfect for indie music and the latest releases in rock and punk music. Meanwhile Japanese craft Shiga Kogen beer is served at the counter.
bigloverecords.jp

02 Tower Records, Shibuya: This shop in Shibuya is generally good for everything from J-pop to reggae but above all it impresses with a selection of classical music.
tower.jp/store/shibuya

03 Disk Union, Shinjuku: Record chain Disk Union's outpost in Shinjuku, which is spread over three floors, is probably the best retailer of jazz records in Tokyo.
diskunion.net

Write stuff

Tokyo is a stationery-lover's dream. Our top-three picks in the city are Ito-ya in Ginza (*ito-ya.co.jp*), Winged Wheel in Jingumae (*winged-wheel.co.jp*) and Shosaikan in Aoyama (*shosaikan.co.jp*).

Things we'd buy
—— Tokyo's top take-homes

Rule number one of any visit to Tokyo: arrive with a half-empty suitcase. By the time you board the flight home you will have filled the space (and you might even need an extra bag).

What could be better than a well-designed product that's crafted by an artisan and made to last? Japan has plenty in that department: handcrafted knives from Gifu, rice bowls by potters in Nagasaki, wooden cups from Hokkaido and cedar lunchboxes from Akita. Drop by stationery shops for smooth writing pens, convenience stores for chocolate bars, pharmacies for the most ingenious hair or face products and fashion retailers for socks and other wardrobe essentials. Here is a selection of items that will make the perfect gifts – or even souvenirs – after your visit to the Japanese capital.

01 Hanatsubaki biscuits
from Shiseido Parlour
parlour.shiseido.co.jp
02 Grace wine from Yamanashi
grace-wine.com
03 Junmai-shu saké from
Matsunami brewery
o-eyama.com
04 Baumkuchen from
Club Harie
clubharie.jp
05 Cedar lunchbox by
Shibata Yoshinobu Shoten
magewappa.com
06 Green-tea KitKat
nestle.jp
07 Milk chocolate by Meiji
meiji.co.jp
08 Seisei ice mould from
Tokyu Hands
tokyu-hands.co.jp
09 Yuzu pepper from
Tokyu Honten
tokyu-dept.co.jp/honten
10 Tongs by Sori Yanagi
d-department.com/jp
11 Kumamon Onigiri rice-ball
mould by Arnest
ar-nest.co.jp
12 Japanese curry from
S&B Foods
sbfoods.co.jp
13 Rice bowls by
Hakusan Porcelain
hakusan-porcelain.co.jp
14 Water jug by Tomihiro
Kaneko from D&Department
d-department.com
15 Butter case with cherry-
wood lid by Noda Horo
nodahoro.com
16 Japanese knife by Kiya
kiya-hamono.co.jp
17 Frying pan from
Kama Asa Shoten
kama-asa.co.jp
18 Wooden cup by
Takahashi Kougei
takahashikougei.com
19 Pot stand by Simplicity
sss-s.jp
20 Incense sticks by Lisn
lisn.co.jp
21 Kutami Uchiwa fan from
D&Department
d-department.com/jp
22 Wind-up radio by Muji
muji.com/jp
23 Heiwa slippers
shop.heiwaslipper.com

01 Photo album by Delfonics
delfonics.com
02 Coloured pens by Pilot
pilot.co.jp
03 Post-its by Stálogy
stalogy.com
04 Leather card case by Brooklyn Museum
brooklyn.co.jp
05 Handwash by Three
aoyama.threecosmetics.com
06 T-shirt from Beams
beams.co.jp

07 Uno hair products by Shiseido
shiseido.co.jp/uno
08 Eye cream by FujiFilm
shop-healthcare.fujifilm.jp
09 Wet face towels by Bioré
biore.com
10 Eye mask by Bioré
biore.com
11 Selection of *tenugui*
(Japanese-style handkerchiefs)
kamawanu.co.jp
12 Socks by Tabio
tabio.com

12 essays
—— Eat, drink
and be merry

1

No half measures
The art of bartending
by Dave Broom,
whisky expert

2

Life in the fast lane
City of choices
by Kenya Hara,
graphic designer

3

Hair today, gone tomorrow
The barber as metaphor
by David Karashima,
literary editor

4

Tailored Tokyo
Japanese menswear
by W David Marx,
writer

5

Those were the days
Growing up in Tokyo
by Kaori Shoji,
journalist

6

Sayonara, sushi
Eating European in Tokyo
by Robbie Swinnerton,
food writer

7

The gaijin's
seven shame-arai
Avoiding gaffes
by Richard Spencer Powell,
Monocle creative director

8

Service included
World-beating hospitality
by Kenji Hall,
Monocle Asia editor at large

9

Dreaming of Tokyo
Dazzling design
by Masamichi Katayama,
interior designer

10

Tuna cheeks, sir?
Eating izakaya-style
by Mark Robinson,
cookbook author

11

Eclectic shock
Architectural anarchy
by Fiona Wilson,
Monocle Asia bureau chief

12

Vinyl nirvana
Record-lovers guide
by Kunichi Nomura,
journalist

*The Japanese
translation
was a touch
ambitious*

ESSAY 01

No half measures
The art of bartending

Some of Tokyo's finest drinking dens are hidden away in nondescript office buildings and unassuming alleyways. Seek them out at your first opportunity: their proprietors' keen dedication to crafting the classics is not to be missed.

by Dave Broom, whisky expert

Attention to detail is what sets Tokyo apart. Food, clothes, electronics, books, paper, luggage, secondhand records – the city specialises in providing the finest examples. Tokyo is home to some of the world's greatest bars but, as the city is vast, I tend to explore one area at a time (rather than spending more time in taxis than at the interesting and important end of an evening's business). An area, for example, such as Ginza.

By day home to shoppers, at night Ginza transforms into a neon-bright pleasure zone. It is the home of Japanese bartending and since Japan is the repository of classic techniques, Ginza is the cocktail world's nexus. The best place to understand this is in Star Bar, run by Hisashi Kishi, the master of the cold, hard, short Ginza approach to drinks. Once a casual question about cocktail-shaking techniques resulted in a 20-minute demonstration in which he moved like a karate grandmaster doing *kata*, showing different moves for different drinks. It showed me how, in Tokyo, every element in a drink has equal importance: the bartender, the quality of the ingredients, the shaker, the glass – and even the ice.

In the West, frozen water is simply used to chill and dilute a drink; in Japan it is an active participant. Another of my mentors, Takayuki Suzuki, now lectures internationally on the Japanese way of ice and how not only its quality is important but also how each type of ice has its own properties. In any great Tokyo bar, huge blocks of clear, pure ice are daily shaved, chipped, cracked, cubed and carved into blocks, balls and diamonds. The ice dictates the shake – and the shake creates the drink.

Star Bar and my other personal favourite, Yokohama's Three Martini, are relatively large establishments. Most of Tokyo's bars are tiny, fitting no more than 15 to 20 people. Invisible during the day, when the city drapes itself in grey and black, at night they emerge in unlikely spaces; clustered in buildings, secreted in basements. I found the Bar Glory in a utilitarian office block in the backstreets of Yokohama, while Aquarium is located within Dunhill's flagship Ginza shop, meaning any self-control is soon lost.

It also means that it is possible to spend an evening in one building, such as the Polestar next to Shimbashi Station. On the second floor is Rock Fish, which makes Tokyo's best whisky highball (frozen Kakubin and cold soda served straight up in a frozen glass with lemon twist). After one you can head to the fourth floor to see Hidetsugu Ueno at his Bar High Five for modern twists on the classics.

Their size means that these bars are often microcosms of their owners' personalities and obsessions. Take whisky:

> *"In the West, frozen water is simply used to chill and dilute a drink; in Japan it is an active participant"*

Ginza highlights
—
01 Star Bar
B1 Sankosha Buidling,
1-5-13 Ginza, Chuo-ku
02 Rock Fish
2F, 26 Polestar Building,
7-2-14 Ginza, Chuo-ku
03 Aquarium
Dunhill Store, 2-6-7 Ginza,
Chuo-ku

while having 200 bottles of single malt to hand may be exceptional in the West, it barely registers in Tokyo. Here there are establishments such as Roppongi's Cask and Yurakucho's Campbelltoun Loch, with ranges running into the thousands.

As this is Tokyo you can specialise even further. Take Shinjuku's Zoetrope, which is dedicated to "Japanese-made, western-style spirits": Japanese rum, gin and, most of all, whisky. If you want to learn about the latter, this is your starting point. If rum is your bag there's Tafia, while for tequila and mezcal there's Agave. In the alleys of Golden Gai, a former red-light district, there are 250-odd miniscule bars within two city blocks. Each one is dedicated to some fixation, be it silent movies or free jazz. I spent one memorable night at a bar dedicated to hard-boiled fiction.

What links the smallest bar in Golden Gai to the finest hotel bar is service. If you walk into a Tokyo bar and ask for a martini, a beer and a glass of water, each drink will be made with the same care. This is the concept of *Ichi-go Ichi-e*: being attuned to the moment. The bartender has one chance to make the best drink they can at the moment you ask for it. The key is the drink, not the ego of the bartender. Knowing this makes you, the drinker, relax. You are in good hands. — (M)

ABOUT THE WRITER: Dave Broom is editor in chief of *Whisky Magazine: Japan*, author of *Whisky: The Manual* and a contributor to numerous other publications on the subject of his favourite tipple.

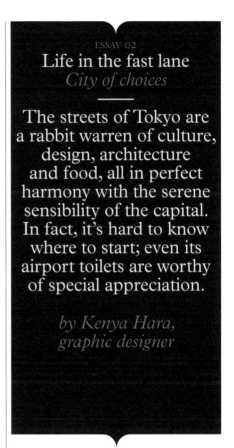

ESSAY 02
Life in the fast lane
City of choices
—
The streets of Tokyo are a rabbit warren of culture, design, architecture and food, all in perfect harmony with the serene sensibility of the capital. In fact, it's hard to know where to start; even its airport toilets are worthy of special appreciation.

by Kenya Hara, graphic designer

The best thing about Tokyo is its Metropolitan Expressway: the **Shutoko**. Smoothly winding its way through Tokyo's residential and skyscraper districts, blithely traversing the city's canals and waterways, this network of high-speed roads is a symbol of what Tokyo had to sacrifice in Japan's period of high economic growth – and what it gained. No other expressway in the world offers such dynamic panoramas. The Central Circular Route in particular gives you stunning views of the urban areas of Tokyo, with an especially thrilling sight of Tokyo Tower from high above.

It has been said that the Japanese are sensitive to small-scale beauty but insensitive to large-scale ugliness; the streets of their capital epitomise this. The Tokyo-Yokohama Metropolitan Area is the largest region of its kind in the world. At first sight it seems a vast mass of misshapen buildings stretching far out to the horizon. But look closely and you'll find a Japanese aesthetic – precision, care, subtlety and simplicity – at work among it all.

There are brilliant Japanese architects too numerous to mention, including winners of the Pritzker Architecture Prize in 2013 and 2014, yet Tokyo's airport buildings are terribly insipid. Why is it that when it comes to the creation of communal space, the city's politicians and public servants seem to completely lack creativity?

That said, on arrival at your chosen airport, take a peek at the toilets. At Haneda they will be perfect; at Narita, pretty good. The Japanese aesthetic certainly makes itself felt in the efforts of cleaning ladies and superintendents, reaching perfection in immaculate toilet bowls. Their gleaming whiteness must be intended to encourage users to leave them as clean and spotless as they found them – and there's a clue here to the best way to enjoy Japan.

With road surfaces sublimely smooth, the result is minimal traffic noise and cars that run along them looking shiny clean. Meticulous attention is given to road design and getting the right dips and rises: the correct gradients for water run-off. When compared to the patched, bumped, potholed roads you find in New York and London, the asphalt pavements around the Marunouchi exit of Tokyo Station are a work of art.

International airline pilots swear that the views of Tokyo city lights at night are the best in the world. And this is more than mere flattery: the luminosity is qualitatively different. You won't find any streetlights that aren't working nor lamps that are dimmer than the rest. Each and every streetlight shines bright and strong, and with exactly the same brightness and strength as all the rest. The net result is seemingly endless, astonishing beauty and depth; the Tokyo city nightscape from the Rainbow Bridge, which crosses northern Tokyo Bay, is to be especially recommended.

Tokyo's residents are not at all narcissistic about their city. The revolution brought by the

"It's said the Japanese are sensitive to small-scale beauty but insensitive to large-scale ugliness; Tokyo's streets epitomise this"

Meiji Restoration just a century and a half ago brought Japanese traditional culture into a head-on clash with that of the West; the result was a chaos that was uncharacteristic and abnormal. That chaos continues and it'll take just a bit more time until we're entirely rid of it. That's why Japanese people assume such a modest air, pricking up their ears at anything new, and why they're so keen to learn things from the rest of the world.

For the same reason our bookshops are always replete with every kind of tome you could desire; just look at the plethora of journals and magazines on the bookshelves in Tsutaya bookshop in Daikanyama. People who are interested in art, architecture or design should look at the books arrayed in On Sundays in the Watari Museum of Contemporary Art in Aoyama. And while we're talking about a huge range of goods, Muji's flagship store in Yurakucho is also a must-see.

If you're into the arts, visit the Nezu Museum in Aoyama, where you'll find superlative Japanese art in a building designed by architect Kengo Kuma. The Japanese-style garden is worth a visit in itself. The Suntory Museum of Art at Tokyo Midtown focuses on classical art in its permanent collection; its temporary exhibits cover contemporary fare.

If you prefer larger collections, the best are at the Tokyo National Museum in Ueno. Toto Gallery Ma in Nogizaka is modestly sized but the exhibits on architecture and design are superb, plus it is associated with the biggest names in Japanese architecture. Gallery 916 in Takeshiba is the place for interesting, off-centre photography exhibits. You should also stop by the Design Gallery on the seventh floor of Matsuya Ginza department store, or visit the Ginza Graphic Gallery. Alternatively, check out 21_21 Design Sight museum in Roppongi.

Bonsai fans will love Uchiku-an in Ginza and for antiques, go to the London Gallery in Roppongi or to Kobijyutsu Kyobashi in Kyobashi. Equally, take a stroll around Kyobashi or Nihonbashi and you'll come across any number of smaller galleries specialising in antique art pieces.

For formal *kaiseki* cooking try Seisoka near Tengenji, Ishikawa in Kagurazaka or Ginza Kojyu in Ginza. For *yakitori* (grilled chicken on skewers), Toritama in Shirokane is great. For curry, try the Murugi Lunch (available all day) at Nair's Restaurant in

Ginza. For sushi, just pluck up the courage and enter any sushi shop with a bold design on the *noren* curtains that hang in the doorway and a white, sparkling clean wooden counter; the fact that there's no price list will add to the thrill. For ramen, just try any shop that has a long queue of people standing outside it.

Use taxis to get around when you're in Tokyo. They're everywhere, they operate all times of day and night and they get you where you want to go smoothly and easily. It might cost you a little more but when you're travelling, time is money.

It's also fun to take a ride on the Tokyo subway system, that tangle of cup ramen noodles that seems to grow ever more squiggly. There's a certain knack to it, though: Tokyo commuters are professionals when it comes to getting on and off trains. Try it a few times but then your best plan? Hop in a taxi and ride that Shutoko. — (M)

ABOUT THE WRITER: Graphic designer Kenya Hara is one of the best-known names in design. He is president of the Japan Design Committee, art director for Muji and professor at Musashino Art University. His Hara Design Institute is both studio and incubator for fresh ideas.

ESSAY 03
Hair today, gone tomorrow
The barber as metaphor

——

A catastrophic self-administered haircut led to an emergency visit to a barber that ultimately became a favourite. Now that it has closed down, does it point to the wider trimming of a generation of Tokyo society?

by David Karashima, literary editor

We all have bad hair days but 17 years ago, the day before I was set to fly back to Boston for my second year of college, I had the worst hair day of my life. My locks felt a little long on the sides but not long enough, I thought, to plump for a professional haircut. Japanese hairdressers could never quite figure out what to do with my half-western hair and the outcome was always unpredictable. So I took my father's trimming comb, leaned over the bathroom sink and ran it through the right side of my head. A clump of hair fell into the sink; when I looked up, I stared at a bald spot that looked like a poor imitation of the Nike swoosh.

My childhood home was in Tokorozawa, just outside of Tokyo, in Saitama Prefecture. As house prices skyrocketed during the bubble economy of the 1980s our family, like many others, was gradually pushed to the outskirts of Tokyo. We ended up in a two-storey house in Tokorozawa, which my parents bought a few months before the economic bubble burst, causing property prices to plummet. The Tokyo-Saitama border near our home was demarcated by the *Yanase-gawa*, a foul-smelling river that carried household waste to the nearby water-reclamation centre. On the worst hair day of my life I remembered that there was a small barber shop on the Tokyo side of this bridge. I biked past Barber Kato all the time and had once even bumped into the tricoloured pole standing next to its door.

Not wanting to head into town with my branded bald spot, I decided to try my luck. Mr Kato, an elderly man with a thick head of hair combed neatly from left to right, didn't raise an eyebrow when I told him that a "friend" had messed up my hair; he simply sat me down on one of the two maroon leather chairs. I insisted that, due to my prominent nose and pointy ears, the obvious solution of shaving off all my hair wasn't a viable option. As such he spent the next hour carefully trimming it, cropping both sides short enough so that the bald spot was barely noticeable but also trying to leave just enough on top so that I didn't end up looking like a Buddhist monk. The final result was far from perfect but given what he had to work with, I thought he had struck a nice balance. As far as I was concerned, Barber Kato was my saviour.

Over the next few years I went to Barber Kato whenever I was back on break from my studies abroad. Even after I moved back to Japan and into

> *"A clump of hair fell into the sink and, when I looked up, I stared at a bald spot that looked like a poor imitation of the Nike Swoosh"*

an apartment in central Tokyo, I would combine visits to my parents with one to Barber Kato. I would sit down in the familiar chair, ask for "the usual" knowing there would be no unpleasant surprises – surely the greatest luxury any hair-grooming establishment can offer – and feel completely at home.

There were three options on Barber Kato's menu: two types of perm priced between ¥8,000 and ¥9,000, and the "Cut" at ¥5,000. While ¥5,000 for a simple haircut seemed a bit steep, Barber Kato appeared to be doing decent business and on weekends the place was always packed with customers from both sides of the Tokyo-Saitama border. It was on perhaps my third or fourth visit that I came to understand the secret of his success. As I momentarily glanced up from the manga comic I was reading, it suddenly dawned on me that every one of the half dozen or so other men in the room were sporting the same hairstyle: the classic barcode combover of the postwar corporate warrior. I realised I was in the presence of not only a seasoned craftsman but a master entrepreneur who had carved out a nice little niche for himself on the outskirts of Tokyo.

Still pretending to read my manga, I observed the master at work. Once seated, the customer would grunt. Barber Kato would nod in response and start working in complete silence. After neatly trimming the back and sides he would swiftly lift the hair on top, take a few centimetres off the end and let it fall gently onto the smooth surface of the scalp. This would be followed by a thorough shave with a straight razor, included in the fee, which always took twice as long as the actual haircut. Once the master was done the customer would grunt his approval and, almost without exception, pay with a crisp ¥5,000 note. The same process was repeated for each and every customer. Barber Kato never missed a step. The whole thing had the feel of a mini assembly line: The Kato Way.

On a recent visit to Tokyo I saw that Barber Kato had closed shop. The two-storey building was still there but the gold letters on the window, the tricoloured pole and Master Kato were gone. I couldn't help but wonder: had Barber Kato, who had been getting on in years, simply decided it was time to hang up his scissors or had changing trends rendered his business model unsustainable? With younger Japanese following the western trend of "going short" when faced with a receding hairline, the barcode warrior was clearly becoming an endangered species.

Whatever the reason, Barber Kato was gone. But what had happened to his customers? Some may have simply passed on but who was now serving the survivors? Were they having to provide step-by-step instructions to hairdressers with no appreciation for The Kato Way? Or, fearing the condescension of younger stylists with no interest in the complex culture that gave rise to this distinct style, were they standing in front of their bathroom mirrors alone, blades held in unsteady hands?

How many Master Katos were we losing each month? How many barcode ronins were roaming the borderlands in search of place, pride and purpose? These were the questions floating through my mind as the "artistic director" at an upscale Aoyama salon served me a soy latte, placed a pile of glossy magazines in front of me and proceeded to give me the second worst haircut of my life. — (M)

ABOUT THE WRITER: David Karashima is an author, translator and editor. He is assistant professor of creative writing at the School of International Liberal Studies, Waseda University, and serves as international editor of *Granta* Japan.

ESSAY 04

Tailored Tokyo
Japanese menswear
———

The elements that make up the capital's fashion scene for discerning gentlemen of all ages are a studied patchwork of foreign influences, Japanese innovation and reimagined styles from decades gone by. What's more, everyone wants a piece of it.

by W David Marx, writer

In the late 20th century, Japanese menswear was a mystery to the West. Unknown to most, it was painfully inaccessible to those who had seen glimpses of its magic. Now, in the age of the internet, Japanese fashion is enjoying the spotlight; street-photo blogs reveal the daily wardrobes of dapper Japanese gentlemen at European fashion shows.

But for all its variety and excellence, the Japanese menswear scene is only about 50 years old and you can learn a lot about it just from a stroll around Tokyo's shopping districts. Until the early 1960s, "dressing up" in Japan meant tailor-made suits in conformist designs. Everything changed in the mid-1960s when Kensuke Ishizu of Van Jacket convinced students to shed their stuffy black woollen uniforms and wear Ivy League campus duds: button-down shirts, chino pants, repp ties and madras sports jackets.

The party started in Ginza, Tokyo's ritziest neighbourhood for most of the 20th century. The kids fell in love with Van Jacket's Ivy style at Teijin Men's Shop near Ginza crossing; so much so that police felt the need to arrest hundreds of youths in trendy clothing in September 1964 to clear the area for the Olympics. Photos from the glory days still hang on the Teijin Men's Shop walls and the shop still offers Ginza's regal gentlemen the finest mix of traditional American and British looks.

Down the street is the Uniqlo flagship, the Japanese brand with the biggest global footprint which has deep roots in 1960s Ivy.

"You can learn a lot about Japanese menswear just from a stroll around Tokyo's shopping districts"

Founder Tadashi Yanai's father ran a Van Jacket store called Men's Shop OS in Yamaguchi Prefecture. Another Van alumnus from Yamaguchi is Yoshio Sadasue, who started traditional shirtmaker Kamakura Shirts to keep the Ivy spirit alive in the shirting world. The brand's Hiroo store Tex Teq makes elegant made-to-measure shirts at prices so low they would be nearly impossible outside of Japan, with the Oxford cloth button-downs highly recommended.

Up the street in Gaienmae is magazine *Free&Easy*'s Rugged Museum, which offers items from traditional brands such as Polo Ralph Lauren as well as an original line of classic US styles. In the late 1960s, a rougher, denim-heavy hippie style displaced Ivy as the primary look for youth. The production of Japanese blue jeans started at the same time in the small town of Kojima in Okayama Prefecture and today many Kojima brands are still pushing towards innovation.

Johnbull Private Labo sells durable workwear with subtle hints of high design in its Harajuku location, while Kapital's two shops in Roppongi Hills subsume you in a world of creative nomads frolicking

Menswear musts
—
01 **Teijin Men's Shop, Ginza**
Old-school American and British fashion.
02 **Johnbull Private Labo, Harajuku**
Jeans, shirts and denim jackets.
03 **Kapital, Roppongi**
Wrinkled cotton meets precision sewing.

around in patched-up garments made from artisanal dyes and precision sewing.

Harajuku emerged as a youth fashion neighbourhood in the 1970s thanks to a completely different style to Ivy and hippie: 1950s rock'n'roll. Bar proprietor Masayuki Yamazaki started Japan's first vintage clothing store, Cream Soda, to sell a pile of old bowling shirts and brothel creepers he picked up at a flea market in London. He soon ran out of stock so instead made his own line of original 1950s-inspired goods. After raking in millions, Yamazaki opened the art deco megastore Pink Dragon on the end of Harajuku's Cat Street in the early 1980s. The American diner and rooftop pool are gone but you can still buy a yellow leopard-skin wallet.

In the second half of the 1970s, Harajuku transformed from rock-glam style to more preppy aesthetics with the opening of the first Beams location in 1976, selling California casual right off the UCLA campus. Within a few years, Beams F was launched to offer the upscale, loafer-loving "trad" of Newport Beach teens. Beams' Harajuku empire is now vast: Beams International Gallery for the latest European designer brands and Beams+ for Ivy, military-inspired outdoor gear and other classic US looks. Members of Beams' management team splintered off in 1989 to open their own store in the form of United Arrows, and today United Arrows Harajuku for Men is one of the city's best spots to pick up a fresh selection of menswear designers both local and global.

While Beams sold new imports, Harajuku's rustic vintage stores Chicago and Voice popped up in the early 1980s to give teens a chance to own antique 501s and ultra-rare Lee Rider Jackets pulled from the basements of decaying general stores in abandoned US towns. Today Banana Boat displays its collection of pricey deadstock jeans behind glass cases, while the basement in Berberjin functions like a museum of Levi's.

In the late 1980s, teens fled Harajuku to buy a more basic US casual style in Shibuya, but the neighbourhood made a comeback in the mid-1990s during the craze for Ura-Harajuku streetwear brands Goodenough, Undercover, A Bathing Ape and Neighborhood. Most of the original Ura-Harajuku shops are now gone but the spirit lives on in nearby Visvim, which applies ancient production techniques to modern designs and cutting-edge materials. Visvim's designer Hiroki Nakamura does what Japanese brands do best: finds a very bright future in the deep archives of the past. — (M)

ABOUT THE WRITER: W David Marx is a writer based in Tokyo who is also the founder and editor of *neojaponisme.com*. His first book, *Ametora: How Japan Saved American Style*, is a cultural history of Japanese menswear.

ESSAY 05

Those were the days
Growing up in Tokyo

Murdered felines, public bathing, graphic war stories and bouts of alfresco intercourse: summer holidays in Tokyo during the Showa Era certainly proved to be memorable affairs.

by Kaori Shoji, journalist

The cat was lying on its side, one eye gouged out. I stared, as one does at 10 years old. It was August in downtown Tokyo and the clammy air enveloped the body like an old shower curtain. Probably this murder was the work of a crow; several of them were leisurely circling the death scene.

I continued to stare and then straightened up to adjust my leather book bag, weighing on my back like a sack of bricks. Supposedly we were in the middle of the summer holidays but on this day – 15 August – we had to go to school to commemorate the Japanese surrender during the Second World War. In 15 minutes' time I would be standing in the hot, dusty schoolyard while the principal went on about people burning to death during the US fire bombings and how the entire downtown district was ash and rubble. Death again. I sent up a prayer that the evil old coot himself would die and put us out of our misery.

Back in the Showa Era, otherwise known as the extremely eventful period

between 1926 and 1989, Tokyo streets were dirty and the stench of struggle was always in the air, especially in the downtown area where my brother and I spent summers with my father's uncle and his wife. They graciously put us up in their apartment, consisting of two six-mat *tatami* rooms and a tiny kitchen. The bath was so small that it was more sensible to frequent the local *sento* or bathhouse, where one jostled for an empty seat in front of the faucets and then soaked in the huge, hot bath.

Naked women went to and fro. Some seemed fantastically old and deformed with age but for the most part they were pathetically thin, their nipples shrivelled at the end of flattened breasts. I thought of the adult women I knew in my neighbourhood back in Brooklyn Heights, New York, and marvelled at the difference. I thought of my friend Darlene, who at the age of 11 had a modelling job. Her tanned, bare-footed, pot-smoking mum wore micro shorts and made brownies for dinner.

These two worlds may as well have been separated by different galaxies yet I belonged to both. For most of the year I lived with my parents and three brothers in a brownstone house in the Heights. My father drove to work over the bridge every morning in a secondhand Oldsmobile to an office in the World Trade Center, where Japanese banks had set up shop. But in June, when schools in the US shut for summer, we children were farmed out to various locales in Tokyo to stay with

---

Recommended neighbourhoods

01 Monzen-Nakacho
A few original canals survive here, where real Tokyoites live.
02 Sumida River
Recently became so clean that the fish have come back.
03 Kokubunji
Leafy and residential with plenty of cafés.

relatives and attend "real Japanese school" for the rest of the summer. My parents were shit-scared of the prospect of us turning into typical American teens, demanding rights and car keys.

My two older brothers stayed with my grandparents in a nice neighbourhood in Kokubunji, a step deemed necessary for their education. My younger brother and I were fielded out to Monzen-Nakacho, way downtown by the Sumida River. Walking to school in the morning I would see the mangled carcasses of rats and frogs on the street while a few metres away, couples who had foregone the love hotel made desperate love in the morning light. Outdoor sex was rampant up until the end of the Showa Era, as was spitting, public urinating and heavy-duty groping on commuter trains. Later I read in *Newsweek* that the Clinton-Lewinsky scandal broke because she had stains on her dress to prove he did it. "Hah – same goes for me and every other girl in Tokyo," I thought.

Now female commuters in Tokyo can ride the "women only" train cars during rush hour. The pavements are clean and bloodless; apartments are more spacious and much more sanitary. Am I the only one who thinks all this is a bit boring? Where's our sense of isolated uniqueness, our legacy of flat-chested poverty? Still, one thing to be thankful for: the principal is finally and very definitely dead. — (M)

"Walking to school in the morning I would see the mangled carcasses of rats and frogs on the street while a few metres away, couples made desperate love in the morning light"

ABOUT THE WRITER: Kaori Shoji honed her NY accent on the mean streets of Brooklyn and her deep knowledge of *shochu* and *yakitori* among the stalls of Isezaki-cho. She writes for various publications in Japan and the US and dreams of becoming the Japanese, female version of Sherlock Holmes.

ESSAY 06
Sayonara, sushi
Eating European in Tokyo

——

Of course you can come to the Japanese capital and eat the finest cuisine that the country has to offer. But you might also want to consider going off-menu to sample the increasing number of French-flavoured delights.

by Robbie Swinnerton, food writer

You don't come to Tokyo to eat French, Italian or Spanish food. Why would you when there is so much great sushi, tempura, teppanyaki and ramen to tempt you? But if you do want a change-up – and a bit of a break from dining on *washoku* 24/7 – you might be surprised at what's on offer; there is cuisine here to match the best there is in Europe.

For decades, young Japanese have headed off to Europe to study the culinary arts, seeking hands-on experience in the kitchens of Michelin-starred maestros. In the old days the aim was to learn classic cuisine – first haute, later nouvelle – and then, once back in Japan, faithfully replicate the techniques and recipes they had learned.

More recently the pattern has changed. A new generation of chefs has emerged with the confidence to develop their own individual styles, marrying French technique with a homegrown Japanese sensibility: a passion for quality ingredients, from *wagyu* beef to the finest seafood; intense devotion to the seasons; exquisite, understated presentation on the plate; and multicourse tasting menus that rival the intricacies of more traditional Japanese *kaiseki* cuisine.

If that sounds much like the template for modern French food, that's because so much inspiration has flowed in the opposite direction, too. Ever since Paul Bocuse began drawing on *kaiseki* as an inspiration for his nouvelle cuisine, the procession of chefs doing the same has not stopped. Alain Ducasse visits Japan constantly (more than 120 times to date) and it's not only because he has restaurants here. For Ducasse and his fellow countrymen – Joël Robuchon and Pierre Gagnaire among them – the aim of their Tokyo restaurants is to replicate the experience of dining in Paris; essentially, to serve their greatest hits. For the new generation of Japanese chefs there are far fewer limiting factors; the result has been an explosion of great and creative gastronomy.

Yoshihiro Narisawa is one chef who has led the way. After training with Bocuse, Robuchon and Frédy Girardet, Narisawa had earned all the necessary credentials and was even earmarked as the opening chef for Robuchon's eponymous chateau restaurant in Ebisu. Instead, Narisawa has followed his own intensely terroir-driven muse. At his self-named restaurant in Aoyama, Narisawa's dishes don't just reflect his local landscape – the

> *"Tokyo may have more Michelin-starred restaurants than any city in the world but some of the more creative chefs remain off the radar"*

earth, woodland and water – they actually contain them. His soil soup (yes, really) is as much of a calling card as his superb black-crusted *wagyu*. These days he even crosses into Japanese territory with delicacies such as deep-fried *fugu* blowfish. Ultimately though the service, wine cellar and dessert trolley that round out his exceptional meals really are unmistakably French.

Leading the pack of younger chefs is Shuzo Kishida, whose sleek, modern restaurant Quintessence has held three stars since the very first Michelin guide to Tokyo in 2008. Formerly sous-chef under Pascal Barbot at L'Astrance in Paris, Kishida clearly acknowledges his debt. But he has also developed a distinctive culinary personality of his own. One item that remains constant year-round on Kishida's menu – even following his move to new, larger premises last year – is his opening appetiser: freshly made goat's milk *bavarois*. Seasoned with sea salt, olive oil and flakes of lily bulb and macadamia nut, it's the kind of dish that is likely to return to you in your dreams.

Tokyo may have more Michelin-starred restaurants than any other city in the world but some of the more creative Japanese French-trained chefs remain off the radar of the *Red Guide*'s inspectors. A case in point: Hiroyasu Kawate, owner-chef of the brilliant Florilège, though that may well change with a recent move into new digs. With his theatrical open kitchen and expanded 13-course tasting menu, his is one of the openings (well, reopenings) of the year thus far.

Favourite restaurants
—
01 Narisawa, Aoyama
2–6–15 Minami Aoyama, Minato-ku
02 Quintessence, Shinagawa
6-7-29 Kita Shinagawa, Shinagawa-ku
03 Zurriola, Ginza
4F, Kojun Building, 6-8-7 Ginza, Chuo-ku

There is outstanding Italian cuisine to be found in Tokyo as well, just as long as you're not looking for full-throttle *cucina della mamma*. Tetsuya Honda, at his namesake restaurant, is a chef who brings subtlety and sophistication to both antipasti and main courses. But it is his delicate pastas – especially his trademark squid-ink *tagliolini* topped with raw sea urchin – that have come to epitomise the genre that is now known as Tokyo-Italian.

Even when it comes to pizza there are a good half-dozen places in the city that can give the *pizzaiolos* of Naples a run for their money. Leading the way is Seirinkan, whose veteran owner Susumu Kakinuma is as idiosyncratic in his cooking as in his decor, and who resolutely refuses to produce any other pizzas than marinara and margherita. Both are well worth crossing town for, mind you.

Spanish food has never captured the imagination of chefs in Japan in quite the same way as Italian or French. However, that did not deter Seiichi Honda from spending four years in San Sebastian discovering the secrets of Basque cooking. Now at the helm of elegant basement restaurant Zurriola, he is producing superlative high-end cuisine. His 12-course dinners are a tour de force and even lunch is a six-course event that calls for a couple of hours – and some really good wine – to do it justice. *Buen provecho*, Tokyo. — (M)

ESSAY 07
The gaijin's seven shame-arai
Avoiding gaffes

────

A visit to Tokyo offers exposure to a cavalcade of cultural delights but it also opens up the distinct potential to fall foul of exacting customs. From tattoos to loo shoes, allow us to advise.

by Richard Spencer Powell, Monocle

After my first visit to Tokyo my stock response to the question, "So, how was it?" went as follows: "It's a mecca for graphic design. If you're a fashion designer you must see Milan; if you're a chef then go to Paris. But for designers, Tokyo is the capital of the world."

That trip, taken over a decade ago, was a client-sponsored research exercise. Indulgent? No, it was money well spent. As a designer I can still reference the sights and delights of that maiden exploration within my work. I've since been back a number of times and I've altered my opinion. Tokyo isn't a mecca for design: it's a scintillating metronome that swings from good fashion to good

ℹ

ABOUT THE WRITER: Robbie Swinnerton arrived in Tokyo 35 years ago in search of sushi, seaweed and artisan soba noodles. Since then he has written extensively on Japanese food and restaurants. His Tokyo Food File column has run in the *Japan Times* since 1998.

design. Tokyo trumps all others at their own game with better fashion than Milan and better food than Paris. It's good to the point of exhaustion and can make you sigh at the perfection of it all. And yet it's not off-putting, it's charming; it's a treasure trove of good.

However, if there is one flaw in this superlative city it's this: as a westerner you soon feel like a clumsy oaf; inept, uncultured and oversized. You never feel more like an outsider than when in Tokyo. The Japanese have a word for us, *gaijin*, which means "foreigner" in a slightly snooty way. So to avoid being too obviously a member of this set, follow these basic rules acquired through a history of embarrassment.

1. Be careful where you tread: Pay heed, wayward westerners: I have fallen foul of several slipper-shoe incidents in Japan. You really don't want your giant canoe shoes ending up where they don't belong – namely on the inside of certain restaurants, particularly the more traditional ones. If your waiter or hostess gestures to your feet it's not to attain the style code of your Nikes. It means: get those dirty boats off before you come in. Calmly slip off your booties and step into a set of house slippers or stay in your socks. (Always, *always* wear nice new socks.) The same rule applies to shop changing rooms: stomping in with an armful of

"As a westerner you soon feel like a clumsy oaf; inept, uncultured and oversized"

T-shirts and yen but with your footwear still on will get a swift reprimand. Shoes off, *gaijin*; don't go soiling the booth for the next, infinitely more civilised customer.

2. Be *really* careful where you tread: In some restaurants where cleanliness hits operating-theatre levels there's a second tier of slipper: the toilet slipper. In such cases you have to come out of your snobby house slipper and put on the loo shoe before entering the WC. For most this number of shoe changes can feel too Imelda Marcos for one evening. Try to remain calm and don't do as I once did: having successfully passed over to the toilet slipper, I forgot to swap back and returned to an immaculate sashimi restaurant wearing the contaminated abominations on my feet. Had there been a long enough blade to hand I think it would have been *sayonara* before the bill.

3. Swimming, rule 1: A luxurious hotel swimming pool is not only for aqua-aerobic jet-lag recovery. It is also a sanctuary of calm order where a *gaijin* novice can find themselves ejected for a variety of dishonourable acts. Don't dive in without a swimming cap and be sure to use the correct shower

procedure before contaminating the pool. Tattoos are taboo in most places – it's deemed far too *yakuza* (organised crime) – so if you've got some ink, best run a bath instead.

4. Swimming, rule 2: Watch your entry. A combination of low light and reflective surfaces can make locating the pool's entry point tricky. I once fell into the Grand Hyatt spa pool because I attempted to enter via a mirage of steps.

5. Taxis: Tokyo taxi doors magically open and close on their own so don't touch them. It will swiftly result in awkwardness paired with a stubbed finger as the door swings out to collide with your hand.

6. Gratuity: Tipping isn't required; in fact it's considered an insult. The Japanese have set up a radical system where everything is charged at what it's worth and not 12.5 per cent less. Simple.

7. Business cards: A yin-and-yang version of a chicken-and-egg scenario. To exchange business cards with someone you have to simultaneously hold your card with both hands while accepting your counterpart's with both hands. To do it perfectly would require four hands. — (M)

ABOUT THE WRITER: Richard Spencer Powell is MONOCLE's creative director. He first visited Tokyo in the 2000s and has returned regularly, be it to direct Monocle fashion shoots or scout for design inspiration.

ESSAY 08
Service included
World-beating hospitality
────

Getting used to the attentiveness of staff in Japan takes time but it helps soften the edges of life lived at a sprint. It could also teach the rest of the world a thing or two about taking pride in going that extra mile.

by Kenji Hall, Monocle

Remember the last time you visited your favourite shop and couldn't find what you were looking for? Maybe you asked the staff for help; maybe the answer wasn't what you were hoping for. "Sorry, we don't have it," they may have said. It's a conversation killer, like being told: "We can't help you."

Which explains why you would never hear this from the staff at that most venerable of Tokyo department stores: Takashimaya. Instead of apologising for not stocking an item they will send you to another store, a rival even, that might have what you want.

One Takashimaya employee famously took the policy a step further: he climbed into a taxi with customers who were from out of town and personally guided them to their destination – and took care of the cab fare. Behind this is the notion that winning loyal customers matters more in the long term. (Those customers from out of town later returned to shop at Takashimaya.)

You don't have to spend much time in Tokyo before realising that Japan wrote the book on hospitality. Everyone seems to be bending over backwards to make sure you're looked after. They're not just unfailingly polite: people genuinely seem eager to help. And nobody works for tips – shocking for an American like me.

I was reminded of the lengths that companies go to one evening during my commute. While transferring subway lines at Kokkai-gijido-mae Station, I noticed two men jogging up the stairs, their navy uniforms marking them as employees of subway operator Tokyo Metro. It would have been faster to take the escalator but Tokyo Metro employees never do, because escalators are there for customers.

The same goes for seats on trains. Even on one that's empty you would never find subway employees in uniform – whether they be conductors or track-maintenance crew – taking the weight off their feet. A little extreme, perhaps, given that a seated employee probably wouldn't bother most people. But these small things matter when you're in a market where consumers are spoilt for choice and somebody is bound to notice.

"You don't have to spend much time in Tokyo to realise that Japan wrote the book on hospitality"

Imagine how enormous training manuals in this country's service sector must be. They tell employees how deeply to bow, how to hold their hands when gesturing, what level of formality to use and how you should never sit down until after a customer has done so.

There is only so much you can teach however, and the downside to all this heavy emphasis on training is that flexibility can take a backseat to doing things by the book. Over the years I have endured my share of robotic, inflexible service. But that is generally the exception. If you go for a trim at The Barber in

Customer satisfaction

01 Expert wrapping
Department stores gift wrap with a single sheet of paper.
02 The handover
Two hands are used to pass your items to you.
03 Departure point
Staff come outside to see you off.

Shibuya and happen to fall asleep, you are unlikely to be roused by the clack of heels on the hardwood floors: the stylists have all been taught to tiptoe around noiselessly in their Oxford shoes.

Aboard the Shinkansen the women who push snack carts down the centre aisle will turn, clasp their hands together and bow as they leave each car – even if everyone's seat is facing the other way and nobody twists around to watch.

When you hop into the back of a black Nihon Kotsu taxi the driver will greet you, introduce himself and thank you for choosing Nihon Kotsu before running the meter. It's second nature for veteran drivers but that's partly because for years they have started every 21-hour shift by reciting in unison what they will say to a customer during a pick-up.

In a city where it can feel like everyone is living on top of each other, having such extraordinary service as the norm makes the place a little bit more liveable. — (M)

ABOUT THE WRITER: Kenji Hall is MONOCLE's Asia editor at large, based in Tokyo. Raised in California, he has lived in the city for more than a decade. His pick for the best Japanese service? Aboard the Shinkansen. You'll witness everything you need to know about the country while hurtling along at 320 km/h.

ESSAY 09

Dreaming of Tokyo
Dazzling design

In those boom years in the middle of the bubble, Japan's capital was a flame that drew the brightest designers to its light. It was the moment the city became the Tokyo of our imaginations; this is how it felt to be there.

by Masamichi Katayama, interior designer

Growing up in the countryside in Okayama there was always a sense that you had to be in Tokyo to get to the starting line. It was as if there was this fascinating train with only one stop: Tokyo. I saw Tokyo on television and in magazines but it felt so far from home. It was like another country. I know I visited Tokyo when I was six but I don't remember it. I went again when I was in high school. Later I took a job selling drinks on the Shinkansen just because it would take me to Tokyo. My first impression was of the number of people and the amazing choice of products available. I remember thinking I wanted to go shopping immediately.

I studied interior design in Osaka and eventually moved to Tokyo. Back then it was a golden age for Japanese fashion, when brands such as Comme des Garçons, Issey Miyake and Yohji Yamamoto were all-powerful. The definition of coolness is different now but those stores were *so* cool

at that time; the epitome of glamour and fashion. I had to muster up the courage just to step inside. There was this atmosphere that some people just understood. It was like a new fashion movement, something really special.

It was also the time of the bubble economy when money was flowing freely and international designers were being invited to do projects here. Japan has fewer architectural restrictions than Europe and the US so they were able to express what they wanted. And people like me were able to watch new design being realised right here. It was like a World Expo of design. I remember works by Philippe Starck, Nigel Coates, Tadao Ando, Mario Bellini, Shiro Kuramata, Shigeru Uchida, Takashi Sugimoto and many more.

Today there is so much design in Tokyo that you have to work even harder to stand out. There are far more shops and retail developments than in other cities. It is incomparable. And yet that provides a lot of opportunities for designers and because of the scrap-and-build attitude there is plenty of scope to experiment. Retail design is everywhere: in freestanding shops, department stores and concessions. Design trends change constantly, just as they do in the fashion business.

"I moved to Tokyo in the golden age of Japanese fashion, when Comme des Garçons, Issey Miyake and Yohji Yamamoto were all-powerful"

I love shopping, especially in Aoyama. Harajuku and Shibuya are good too. For anyone interested in retail design, Aoyama and Harajuku are like walk-through histories of the modern era. I also love to see Japanese architecture that couldn't have been built anywhere else: St Mary's Cathedral or Yoyogi National Gymnasium by Kenzo Tange. Or the Edo-Tokyo

Shop style

01 Antiques Tamiser
Idiosyncratic Ebisu antique shop with a rare eye.
02 Loopwheeler
Wonderwall-designed shop for classy sweats and hoodies.
03 Post
Bibliophile's dream, selling books by only one publisher at a time.

Open-Air Architectural Museum, where you can see Kunio Maekawa's own house. There are many places that are inimitably "Tokyo": Takeshita Street, Akihabara, the neon in Shinjuku, even a packed train. There is so much to discover.

When I first came to this city, design offered a new vision that went hand in hand with what was happening in fashion, social trends, dining and nightclubs. I remember thinking to myself that it seemed unreal, as if it was happening far away or I was watching it all unfold on television. Tokyo wasn't so connected to the rest of the world at that time but the city made its own movement. It was something that was local but huge at the same time.

Design is a widely accepted part of everyday life now but I don't think we feel the same level of excitement. In my mind the power of design was defined back then in that golden age. Design, space and what was happening in that space: all of those elements together created the magic. That's where it all started for me and ever since I have wanted to surpass it. — (M)

ABOUT THE WRITER: Masamichi Katayama is an interior designer and principal of Wonderwall. He is also a professor at Musashino Art University. Through his work on such projects as Uniqlo's global flagship shops and Intersect by Lexus, Katayama has come to define modern Japanese retail design.

ESSAY 10
Tuna cheeks, sir?
Eating izakaya-style

If you want an authentic dining experience in Tokyo you should look no further than an 'izakaya': a relaxed haven of the purest Japanese ingredients. Be sure to bring an open mind and an empty stomach.

by Mark Robinson, cookbook author

The first thing you do on entering this quintessentially Japanese space is sit down, either at a cosy counter or an invariably cramped table, and order a beer. Wine, saké and shochu come later. Welcome to the robust, savoury heart of Japanese casual dining: the *izakaya*.

An *izakaya* – otherwise known as a Japanese tavern or rough equivalent to a Spanish tapas bar – will always be noisy with diners. Near your seats, conveniently placed hooks and baskets accommodate your coats and bags. Chairs, if you're using them, will be tiny. Your shoes – if you're sitting on a raised *tatami*-mat area around low tables – will be stored in small lockers or lined up at the *tatami* edge, as if at a children's sleepover; there are communal slippers to wear to the bathroom. A waiter will bring hot or cold hand towels and a small appetiser. The bustle of the open kitchen and the sight of happy red-faced patrons at the counter complete the scene.

The beauty of *izakaya* is that there is something for everyone, whether it's fermented seafood or fried chicken. If the menu isn't up on the walls it is often handwritten in characters on a photocopied sheet. You keep it close throughout the meal. Nearly all of the offerings are small dishes made for sharing. In many *shitamachi*, or downtown places, they emerge from a kitchen perhaps no bigger than a closet. One of the best menu guides is to cast an eye over what other diners are having. Some of it will be challenging, like pickled squid guts. But prices are low so it is easy to experiment.

The menu may be divided between fresh fish of the day (in styles from sashimi to grilled or even simmered), deep-fried things, meat (perhaps broiled on skewers or slow-cooked), salads, and rice things including pickles and miso soup. In the likely event that it's all in Japanese it becomes handy to know the names of some dishes, point to the next table or leave it to the house: say, "*Omakase onegaishimasu*," then work out

Keep it casual
—
01 **Kanae, Shinjuku** Homely gastropub with speciality saké menu.
02 **Shinsuke, Yushima** Home-style cooking and old-fashioned ambience.
03 **Uoshin, Nogizaka** Fresh fish and hearty atmosphere.

a price. There will always be daily specials, too. Order a handful of items to get yourself going and then order again – and again if you like – throughout the evening. Perhaps start with sashimi as it tastes better before heavier flavours cloud the palate.

As the evening progresses you will find dishes previously unnoticed begin catching your eye. A Japanese meal traditionally wraps up with something starchy. You may consider *zosui* (a sort of porridge of eggs and rice) or perhaps a refreshing serve of chilled noodles. But there really are no rules.

No one knows who ran Japan's first *izakaya* but historians believe the eating style took off after alcohol shops began offering food well over a century ago. *Izakaya* can be big or small; some chain establishments seat more than 100. A key to the experience is the sense of intimacy and closeness. If you are seated at the counter you may be almost within touching distance of the people who prepare your food. These small counters and tables will position you right alongside your fellow diners. The proprietor, often an owner/chef, may be close by.

This sense of proximity extends to the environment as well. Local fish and vegetables connect you with the seasons. Many traditional *izakaya* are situated in old houses in which the master lives upstairs or at the back. Such a set-up makes these *izakaya* much more than just restaurants: they play a neighbourhood role as locals become regulars, not unlike the western bar or pub.

"Cast an eye over what other diners are having. Some of it will be challenging, like pickled squid guts. But prices are low so experiment"

When Unesco listed Japanese food as an intangible cultural heritage asset in 2014, Japanese commentators met the news with great fanfare. Finally, they said, experts had acknowledged this cooking for its beautiful presentation, health benefits, freshness and technique. But what the recognition also hinted at was that by the nature of its uniqueness, Japanese food is a difficult thing to grasp.

European cooks, or those from other Asian countries, emphasise the addition of flavour. The Japanese cook, on the other hand, aims to find the freshest ingredient, remove any bitterness and present it as it is. For example, the popular *izakaya* dish Onion Slice is exactly that: finely sliced raw onions, quickly refreshed in vinegar and sprinkled with soy sauce. Japanese food is more about subtraction.

This can create dissonance when international foodies visit highly rated traditional *kaiseki* haute-cuisine restaurants. They may expect the pyrotechnics of French, Thai or Chinese. But Japanese food is not a knockout experience; if there is anything about it that is sublime it may come from the bigger picture. How this food gently fits the environment; how, through the essence of *konbu* seaweed broth, wild mushrooms, or ayu river fish you are eating the sea, the forests or the streams. In this sense, high-level Japanese cuisine may be the original molecular cooking.

The *izakaya*, with its relaxed surroundings and vast range of simple dishes, can be an ideal bridge between this kind of purism and casual dining. One of my favourite *izakaya* in central Tokyo has this spirit. Nakamura Shokudo occupies the utilitarian premises of a former cooking school, complete with angled mirrors over the kitchen area. The concept is of a Japanese-western diner or cafeteria. The menu ranges freely across boundaries, including cabbage rolls, meatballs and deep-fried chicken.

On one particularly memorable evening there was a crisp salad of coriander leaves with finely sliced green pepper and a dressing of sesame and Thai fish sauce *naam pla*. There was also lightly battered burdock-root tempura, tuna cheeks sautéed with black pepper and, to finish, cold Chinese noodles with sesame sauce.

The head chef had also just unveiled his new menu addition: meat pies. Small, plump filo pastries containing a sort of tomato mince. Hardly a Japanese dish but the unforced eclecticism and sense of exploration sum up the best of *izakaya*.

The Japanese expression *"Ho-tto suru"* describes an exhalation of relief. That's how I feel about *izakaya* dining. Bound by no rules yet operating within a clearly defined form, it is a feeling like coming home. — (M)

ⓘ

ABOUT THE WRITER: Mark Robinson was born in Tokyo and moved to Sydney aged two. He returned in his mid-twenties and is the author of *Izakaya: The Japanese Pub Cookbook*. He chronicles his riverside neighbourhood at *ginzaline.com*.

ESSAY 11
Eclectic shock
Architectural anarchy
——
As capitals go, Tokyo is remarkably – not to say alarmingly – nonchalant about its architectural heritage. Significant buildings regularly vanish but the city remains a treasure trove of the experimental and daring.

*by Fiona Wilson,
Monocle*

To love Tokyo you have to set aside the aesthetic rules that apply to most other cities. Old buildings? Most have been taken out by earthquakes, fires and the ferocious bombing that pummelled Tokyo during the war. Look at aerial views of the city in 1945 and you might think you are looking at Hiroshima, so total was the destruction in some areas. The Emperor hails from an ancient lineage but his palace was built in the 1960s. Meiji Shrine, an elegant Imperial Shrine in Harajuku, looks historic but it is a postwar rebuild from 1958.

Grand architectural schemes? Hardly. Tokyo never had a Haussmann to straighten it all out and is all the better for it. The city has developed haphazardly and is a fantastic jumble of residential, business and industrial buildings. Go to the east side of the city in particular and small workshops still rumble alongside houses and schools. Tedious zoning rules don't apply in Tokyo. There are no rows of neat terraced housing here either. Look closely and you'll notice the small gap that separates adjacent buildings – another Tokyo quirk.

There are rules about not blocking others' sunlight, which accounts for some of the bizarre architectural contortions, but not about the style or exterior. Can there be a more architecturally varied city? Once you get into the swing of it, it's an exhilarating free-for-all. When someone does complain about the look of a building in Tokyo it comes as a surprise. The poor Italians once came a cropper when they unveiled a new cultural centre. Its bold red colour was intended to recall a Shinto shrine but others didn't see it that way and the *Yomiuri Shimbun* newspaper called the building "grotesque".

Dynamism is a good thing but it can be frustrating that Tokyo's residents are so unsentimental about their architectural legacy. The Empress's family home was torn down with only the slightest of opposition. There was a mild kerfuffle over the outrageous demolition of the Hanezawa Garden, a stunning Taisho-era house that was replaced with a boring residential development, but nothing to unduly trouble the developers. And what other city would have torn down a 1923 hotel designed by Frank Lloyd Wright and replaced it with a nondescript tower block?

Architectural merit is not the issue. The Hotel Okura is a modernist treasure unmatched by any other hotel in the world but that hasn't been enough to save it from being redeveloped by its owners. The western notion of listing a building simply doesn't apply but some have been lucky enough to have a saviour. Tokyo's prewar Central Post Office was due to be flattened

> *"What other city would have torn down a hotel designed by Frank Lloyd Wright and replaced it with a nondescript tower block?"*

until a politician stepped in. It's a façade now (façadism is often a sad compromise) but it's still there. Let's be thankful that Tokyo station didn't go that way. Instead it was painstakingly renovated and the city will be glad it saved this redbrick landmark.

Look at old maps of Tokyo and you'll see that the footprint of historic Edo is still largely in place today. The physical relics might have gone but the sense of history lives on in the people and the city's traditions. In the summer, shrine *matsuri* (festivals) take place all over the city as they have for hundreds of years. Japanese tend to be reticent when it comes to talking about themselves but you have to hope someone is recording their stories. First stop should be 100-year-old Ichiro Sekiguchi, owner of a Ginza coffee shop, who can remember the 1923 Great Kanto Earthquake like it happened yesterday. He is living history.

The city is indifferent to conventional notions of perfection. How can you not love the tumbledown old house that sits defiantly in the nook of the LVMH building on Omotesando? The luxury group simply built around the recalcitrant owner. Wonderful, thrilling, messy Tokyo is an affront to architectural conformity and three cheers to that. — (M)

ABOUT THE WRITER: Fiona Wilson is MONOCLE's Asia bureau chief and has loved Tokyo from the minute her plane touched down. Never having had a car in the city means she has walked its length and breadth – and seen many buildings demolished and many new ones go up in the process.

ESSAY 12

Vinyl nirvana
Record-lovers guide

Tokyo's vintage addicts are legendary but its record collectors are an especially dedicated bunch. Our expert vinylist has tips up his sleeve for the visitor, from the best shops to a bar that will get you in the groove.

by Kunichi Nomura, journalist

Vinyl vanguards

01 Jet Set, Shimo-kitazawa
All-round selection plus well-curated secondhand vinyl.
02 Lighthouse Records, Shibuya
Vinyl techno, house and disco.
03 Reco-fan, Shibuya
Discounted new and used vinyl and secondhand CDs in all genres.

During the 1980s and 1990s, cash-rich Japanese buyers were flying all over the world to buy vintage Levi's, guitars, records, cars and everything else they could get their hands on. Now that the exchange rate is not so favourable, those same items that have been circulating on the domestic market for years are being sold back to international travellers who come to Tokyo. I feel a pang of sadness to see them go even though they're not mine but I guess it's true that what goes around comes around.

One of the best things to buy in Tokyo is vinyl. Seriously: it's the only music format whose sales are increasing. Records are even popular with kids who didn't grow up with them. It's fun to look at the cover, they're nice to touch and the sound is amazing. Tokyo is the mecca for vinyl-lovers from around the world. You probably know that we Japanese can be nerds when it comes to collecting. We like to classify everything in order: by era,

producer and label. Every genre of music is available here and there are enough nerds devoted to each of them to keep all these small secondhand record shops in business. It's dangerous for me to kill time walking around Shibuya or Shinjuku. I always end up in a record shop and suddenly half the day is gone: Disk Union, Reco-fan, Jet Set and Lighthouse Records. The list goes on.

When you walk out of the shop you usually feel like going to a café or bar where they play records, too. If you are in Shibuya, there is a place where the beer is cheap and the record collection mind-blowing: JBS – or Jazz, Blues, Soul – has more than 10,000 records. This small bar is equipped with vintage 1960s Thorens TD124 turntables, a Mark Levinson tube preamp and Altec Lansing speakers, also from the 1960s. For a vinyl experience with a bar tab that won't break the bank, it's the best around. And don't be surprised if you bump into a few well-known international DJs or musicians drinking beer, listening to records and having the time of their lives. — (M)

ABOUT THE WRITER: Born and raised in Tokyo, Kunichi Nomura works as a freelance editor and writer for several magazines, including *Brutus*. He is also an interior designer (he did The North Face Standard shops) and has a DJ team called Mild Bunch. He is currently the creative director of *Studio Voice* magazine when not hosting the J-Wave radio programme *Travelling Without Moving*.

Culture
—— Something
for everyone

There is no excuse to be bored in Tokyo. This is a city with a rich cultural scene to match its long history. Whether you're after high or low art, *kabuki* or karaoke, stadium rock or smoky jazz, it's all here.

Japan is a country of niche interests and there is something for everyone. If manga and anime are your bag you have found your second home. If you're craving more traditional arts you will find the finest museums and the most exquisite Japanese theatre. Music lovers will appreciate the encyclopaedic record shops, while literary types can spend hours browsing in bookshops.

Print media is alive and kicking in Japan – you only have to look at the thousands of magazines on the shelves for proof. Tokyo is also home to the world's two highest-circulation newspapers: the *Yomiuri Shimbun* and *Asahi Shimbun*. Not to mention the world's number one financial daily, the *Nikkei*.

Cinemas
Picture perfect

①
Yebisu Garden Cinema, Ebisu
Classic remake

There are many multiplexes in Tokyo showing the latest Japanese and Hollywood blockbusters but if you're looking for something more offbeat, you could try this little cinema in Yebisu Garden Place. Located next door to the startlingly ersatz chateau that houses Joël Robuchon's Michelin-starred French restaurant, Yebisu Garden Cinema recently reopened after a stint as a venue for live Korean pop.

New owner United Cinemas called on Tokyo architecture firm Intentionallies to remodel the interior. There are now photos on the walls, books to browse and a menu that include cupcakes and wine by the glass. The two screens show a roster of smaller films from around the world. Note that foreign-language films in Tokyo are subtitled in Japanese, not English.
Yebisu Garden Place, 4-20-2 Ebisu, Shibuya-ku
+81 (0)570 783 715
unitedcinemas.jp/yebisu

Silver screen
——
Yebisu Garden Cinema has a cosy feel

Three more cinemas

01 **Uplink, Kamiyama:** This film-distribution company runs three small cinemas showing a selection of independent films. *uplink.co.jp*

02 **Le Cinéma, Shibuya:** Two-screen cinema attached to the Bunkamura cultural centre in Shibuya. *bunkamura.co.jp*

03 **Toho Cinemas, Roppongi:** If you want to see a blockbuster, this ticks the boxes. *tohotheater.jp*

Tokyo on film

01 **Stray Dog, 1949:** Legendary director Akira Kurosawa captured the steamy atmosphere of summer in Tokyo in this tale of an inexperienced policeman (Toshiro Mifune) whose gun is taken by a pickpocket.

02 **You Only Live Twice, 1967:** This exceptionally stylish 007 outing was shot on location in Japan. There are great scenes of James Bond (Sean Connery) on the streets of Ginza, at the sumo stadium and racing through Tokyo in a Toyota 2000GT with fellow spy Aki (Akiko Wakabayashi).

03 **Lost in Translation, 2003:** Scarlett Johansson and Bill Murray made a beguiling couple in director Sofia Coppola's film. Shot on location, mostly in the Park Hyatt hotel, the movie conveys the thrill and occasional bafflement of a first visit to the city.

Museums
Exhibition spaces

Mori Art Museum, Roppongi
Cultural big hitter

This contemporary-art museum opened with great fanfare in the giant Roppongi Hills development in 2003. Although its own collection is small, the museum has enjoyed the clout to curate significant exhibitions of Japanese, Asian and international art. The museum was recently renovated to upgrade facilities and repair the wear and tear caused by millions of visitors.

The museum is open until 22.00 (except Tuesdays) and is worth combining with a trip to the observation deck for views of Tokyo. Visitors to the city should also consider getting a Grutto Pass, which gives free or discounted one-time entry to about 80 museums and galleries. It costs ¥2,000 and is valid for two months. *53F, Roppongi Hills Mori Tower, 6-10-1 Roppongi, Minato-ku +81 (0)3 5777 8600 mori.art.museum/eng*

Of course, I could just fly towards it

Watari-um Museum of Contemporary Art, Gaienmae
Landmark vision

Designed by Swiss architect Mario Botta on a triangular slice of land, this small but influential museum has become a Tokyo landmark with its varied and intriguing exhibitions. Also worth a visit is museum shop On Sundays. *3-7-6 Jingumae, Shibuya-ku +81 (0)3 3402 3001 watarium.co.jp*

③
Mingeikan, Komaba
Everyday art

A must for anyone interested in Japanese crafts, the Mingeikan was founded by Soetsu Yanagi (father of designer Sori Yanagi) in 1936. Yanagi was the leading light of the *mingei* (folk craft) movement that celebrated the art of everyday crafts such as ceramics, glass, basket-weaving and textiles.

The Mingeikan sits on a quiet street in Komaba, housed in a building designed by Yanagi, with a more modern wing attached. Inside, the display cases show *mingei* works from Japan and abroad. It's a treat to remove your shoes at the door and walk across the wooden timbers. *Mingei* has come into vogue in recent years as a younger generation begins to value its craft heritage. Yanagi's home, which was completed a year before the museum, is across the road and open a few days a month.
4-3-33 Komaba, Meguro-ku
+81 (0)3 3467 4527
mingeikan.or.jp

Craft service
—
Folk art is displayed in the Mingeikan

④
Nezu Museum, Aoyama
Traditional treats

The privately run Nezu Museum
opened in 1941 in the home of
industrialist and art collector
Kaichiro Nezu and now occupies
a 2009 building on the same site
designed by architect Kengo
Kuma. Its collection of Japanese
and Chinese art is outstanding
and the new building has brought
a fresh audience to what was once
a well-kept secret. The rebuild is
impressively discreet: a bamboo
corridor leads to a space with a low
sloping roof and picture windows.

Highlights of the collection
include Ogata Korin's famous
18th-century folding screens that
are decorated with irises and
shown each spring for just one
month. The large garden, dotted
with stone lanterns and traditional
wooden tea houses, draws
kimono-clad tea practitioners
from all over Japan.
6-5-1 Minami Aoyama, Minato-ku
+81 (0)3 3400 2536
nezu-muse.or.jp

Nezu
Museum highlights
———
01 Wisteria Screen, Maruyama
Okyo (1733-1795)
02 Lacquer writing box with
deer, 15th century
03 Nachi Waterfall, Shinto scroll
painting, 13th to 14th century
04 Kimono with chess design,
17th century
05 Sheep-shaped bronze,
11th-13th century
BC

National treasure
—
Nezu Museum is impressively discreet

⑤
Ukiyo-e Ota Memorial
Museum of Art, Harajuku
Uniquely Japanese

Back when *ukiyo-e*, or woodblock
prints, were underappreciated as
collectible art works in Japan,
many fine pieces went abroad.
Seizo Ota V did his bit to keep
works by Hokusai, Hiroshige and
dozens of other woodblock artists
in Japan by building a collection of
14,000 prints over the course of
half a century. They are now on
display at this small two-storey
museum that opened on a
Harajuku back street in 1980.

The works are fragile so displays
change every month. That means
you might not glimpse all the
greatest hits on a single visit but
you can be sure there will always
be something worth seeing. The
museum's basement shop is run
by Kamawanu, maker of
printed-cotton *tenugui* cloths.
1-10-10 Jingumae, Shibuya-ku
+81 (0)3 3403 0880
ukiyoe-ota-muse.jp

Printers, inc.
──
'Ukiyo-e'
dates back to
the early 17th
century

6

Taro Okamoto Memorial Museum, Aoyama
Monumental views

Sculptor Taro Okamoto's house, where he lived from 1954 until his death in 1996, is now a museum dedicated to his work. Okamoto's often monumental pieces, such as the giant Tower of the Sun that he made for the 1970 Osaka Expo, are instantly recognisable. The museum holds drawings and sketches for many of his works.

The house is a draw in itself, built by architect Junzo Sakakura, Okamoto's friend and a favourite pupil of Le Corbusier. It is also home to tea shop A Piece of Cake.
6-1-19 Minami Aoyama, Minato-ku
+81 (0)3 3406 0801
taro-okamoto.or.jp

7

Fumiko Hayashi Memorial Hall, Shinjuku
Literary shrine

You don't need to be familiar with the work of novelist Fumiko Hayashi to appreciate her former home in Ochiai in Shinjuku. Hayashi was so determined to get the details right that she took her designer to Kyoto to study architecture. The effort paid off in the form of double-layer cupboards with sliding doors, *shoji* paper screens, neatly crafted wooden drawers and a garden of maple trees and camellias. Hayashi lived here from 1941 until her death in 1951.
2-20-1 Nakai, Shinjuku-ku
+81 (0)3 5996 9207
regasu-shinjuku.or.jp/rekihaku/
fumiko/12

8

Hara Museum, Shinagawa
Independent trailblazer

When Toshio Hara decided to open one of Japan's first contemporary-art museums more than 30 years ago he didn't have a collection. But he did have a unique location: his grandparents' Bauhaus-style villa in Shinagawa (*pictured, above and top*), built by Jin Watanabe in 1938. The museum opened in 1979 and has become an institution where careers are forged and reputations sealed.

Unfettered by corporate obligations, Hara follows his instincts and is never swayed by big names or grand projects. Sophie Calle, Yoshitomo Nara and Olafur Eliasson have all exhibited here and the programme covers all manner of media, nationalities and ages. Comfortably small in scale, the museum also has a shop, garden and a café, which which was built by Arata Isozaki, who also built the Hara's rural outpost in Gunma.
4-7-25 Kita Shinagawa, Shinagawa-ku
+81 (0)3 3445 0651
haramuseum.or.jp

9

Idemitsu Museum of Arts, Hibiya
Theatrical experience

Before you enter the museum, which exhibits the collection of petroleum company Idemitsu Kosan, take a look at the building. The Imperial Theatre – Japan's first western-style performance space – has been here since 1911; the current building dates from 1966 and was designed by Yoshiro Taniguchi, who was also the architect of the Hotel Okura.

Exhibitions change seasonally and are drawn from company founder Sazo Idemitsu's collection. Among the 15,000 pieces are Asian art works – including Japanese paintings and calligraphy as well as ceramics from Japan and China – and paintings by western luminaries such as Georges Rouault.

It's worth taking a breather in the lounge, which overlooks the Imperial Palace. When you've finished, look next door at the Dai-ichi Mutual Life Insurance Building that served as the headquarters for the US military after the war. Supreme commander General MacArthur's panelled office is still there, although sadly not open to the public.
9F Teigeki Building,
3-1-1 Marunouchi, Chiyoda-ku
+81 (0)3 5777 8600
idemitsu.co.jp/museum

Still life
—
Asakura's home features many of his sculptures

Commercial galleries
Art and soul

①

Gallery Koyanagi, Ginza
Trailblazer

Atsuko Koyanagi almost followed in the steps of her father, the fifth-generation owner of a high-end ceramics shop; she initially ran a ceramics gallery but later switched to contemporary art.

Her Gallery Koyanagi occupies the eighth floor of a concrete building on the same plot of land where she grew up. She exhibits the work of about 30 global artists, including that of photographer Hiroshi Sugimoto, media artist Ryoji Ikeda and the Danish-Icelandic artist Olafur Eliasson.
*8F, Koyanagi Building,
1-7-5 Ginza, Chuo-ku
+81 (0)3 3561 1896
gallerykoyanagi.com*

⑩

Asakura Sculpture Museum, Yanaka
Open house

Sculptor Fumio Asakura's home and studio in Yanaka are a delight. He moved there in 1907 then spent years extending the house. There are two wings and a leafy Japanese garden; you can tour the property and discover his sculptural work.
*7-18-10 Yanaka, Taito-ku
+81 (0)3 3821 4549
taitocity.net/taito/asakura*

An artist should always be present in his work

②
IMA Concept Store, Roppongi
Promoting photography

Commercial photography gallery,
café and bookshop rolled into one,
IMA Concept Store's mission is to
introduce the public to up-and-
coming Japanese and international
names who might not be shown in
the more established galleries.

Kohei Nawa took charge of the
interior and the display changes
regularly. There are workshops by
big names such as Takashi Homma
and Daido Moriyama. The shop,
magazine and online site are backed
by Amana, a stock-photo company
whose president Hironobu Shindo
is doing his bit to promote photo
culture in Japan.

3F, Axis Building,
5-17-1 Roppongi, Minato-ku
+81 (0)3 5572 7144
imaconceptstore.jp

In the frame
—
IMA supports
rising talent
in Japan

THREE NAMES TO BUY:
01   Nerhol: Two-man art director/
sculptor unit who make
photographic portraits carved
out of thick layers of paper.
02   Sohei Nishino: Stunning
city landscapes made up of
hundreds of small images.
03   Naoki Ishikawa: Celebrated
mountaineering photographer
who has turned his lens on
Mount Fuji and many of
Japan's further-flung corners.

New Tokyo Contemporaries

They have appointed themselves the New Tokyo Contemporaries but in Tokyo's art world they are also collectively known as the second generation. They are made up of seven galleries that started in the early to mid-2000s and whose owners cut their teeth at some of Tokyo's best-known contemporary-art venues: Scai the Bathhouse, Mizuma Art Gallery, Tomio Koyama and Röntgenwerke.

Since 2008 they have collaborated and hosted events together, featuring the work of emerging artists to target a younger Tokyo audience interested in collecting on a more modest budget.

In a country where homes are small and space for displaying paintings, photographs and sculpture is limited, there hasn't been a huge demand for contemporary art. But after a decade in business these young gallery owners have consolidated their place in the market.
newtokyocontemporaries.com;
aoyamahideki.com;
arataniurano.com;
zenshi.com;
takeninagawa.com;
misakoandrosen.com;
mujin-to.com;
yukasasaharagallery.com

Taka Ishii Gallery, Sendagaya
Picture this

Opened in 1994, Taka Ishii's gallery is a leading venue for photography, film and paintings. With two galleries in Tokyo, one in Paris and another in New York, Ishii is now firmly established as one of the foremost champions of Japanese photography.

He showcases the work of Daido Moriyama, Nobuyoshi Araki and Naoya Hatakeyama, along with such artists as Luke Fowler and Thomas Demand. In mid-2015 he moved one of his galleries from Kiyosumi to Kitasando on the west side of town.
B1F, 3-10-11 Sendagaya,
Shibuya-ku
takaishiigallery.com

Tomio Koyama Gallery, Sendagaya
Big in Japan

Tomio Koyama is celebrated for introducing many of the leading figures in Japan's contemporary art scene, Takashi Murakami, Yoshitomo Nara and Rieko Otake among them.

Koyama deserves credit for expanding the market for contemporary art in a country where, up until a couple of decades ago, there were few buyers. He has used his status to bring more attention to other gallery owners, some of whom moved with him to Kiyosumi, east Tokyo. He recently shifted his main gallery to a basement space shared with Taka Ishii Gallery in Kitasando.
B1F, 3-10-11 Sendagaya, Shibuya-ku
tomiokoyamagallery.com

① Baseball, Gaienmae
Home run

Baseball is huge in Japan. High-school boys dream of winning the nationwide school tournament (*Koshien*) and everyone follows the fortunes of their team in the professional league (*Puroyakyu*).

You don't have to love or know anything about baseball to enjoy a game at Jingu Stadium, the home of the Tokyo Yakult Swallows. It's worth ordering a beer: it is served by beer girls who supply spectators from a tank strapped to their back. If the Swallows hit a home run, expect the fans to pull out mini umbrellas and break into song. The other Tokyo team, the Yomiuri Giants, play indoors in Tokyo Dome to a packed home crowd.
3-1 Kasumigaokamachi, Shinjuku-ku
+81 (0)3 3404 8999
jingu-stadium.com

②

Sumo, Ryogoku
Ring cycle

Top sumo wrestlers (*rikishi*) are
major stars in Japan, as much as
any other modern celebrity. Don't
miss the chance to see them in
action in the ring (*dohyo*).

There are three annual Grand
Sumo tournaments in Tokyo –
January, March and September
– which are held at the impressive
Kokugikan Stadium in Ryogoku.
Tournaments last for two weeks
and wrestlers fight every day in
reverse order of ranking.

Sumo is an exceptionally
ritualised and hierarchical sport,
closely entwined with Shintoism.
The *dohyo* has a shrine-like roof,
salt is thrown by wrestlers for
purification and the judge in the
ring wears the hat and robes of a
Shinto priest. As with any sport, the
more you see, the more involving it
becomes. One thing is clear: size
doesn't trump skill.
*1-3-28 Yokozuna, Sumida-ku
+81 (0)3 3623 5111
sumo.or.jp*

Fighting talk
——
Sumo is a
thrilling and
unique
sport

Theatre/performing arts
Public entertainment

①

Takarazuka Revue, Hibiya
Ladies night

How to explain the phenomenon that is Takarazuka? Essentially it is an all-female theatrical company that performs over-the-top Broadway-style musicals to an audience that is made up almost entirely of women.

Takarazuka, based in the town of the same name in Hyogo Prefecture, has been running since 1914 and its popularity is still going strong. Crowds gather outside the Takarazuka Theatre at the start of the day as the stars arrive and wait patiently to hand over gifts to their favourite performers.

Seats for shows such as the classic *The Rose of Versailles* (an adaptation of a popular manga) are hard to come by but you can still visit the gift shop – packed with DVDs and memorabilia – to get a good idea of just how popular Takarazuka is.
1-1-3 Yurakucho, Chiyoda-ku
+81 (0)3 5251 2001
kageki.hankyu.co.jp

②

National Theatre of Japan, Hanzomon
Traditional arts centre

The showcase for Japan's theatrical arts, the National Theatre is housed in an elegant building designed by Hiroyuki Iwamoto in 1966. There are two stages, showing everything from *kabuki* (drama) and *bunraku* (puppetry) to *buyo* (traditional dance) and *gagaku* (Japanese court music). Performances here are top quality and if you're lucky you might see a Living National Treasure on stage. Don't worry if you don't speak Japanese: simultaneous English translation is available through an earpiece.
4-1 Hayabusa-cho, Chiyoda-ku
+81 (0)3 3265 7411
ntj.jac.go.jp

③

National Noh Theatre, Sendagaya
Ancient mysteries

Noh – which is thought to come from the word for "skill" – is one of the oldest theatrical forms in the world and has been performed in Japan for centuries. It is nothing like western theatre: characters are masked, movements are slow and stylised and the musical accompaniment is a chanting chorus.

Noh is also a level playing field since even Japanese speakers find the language challenging. It is performed at venues across the city and the outdoor performances by torchlight crackle with atmosphere.
4-18-1 Sendagaya, Shibuya-ku
+81 (0)3 3423 1331
ntj.jac.go.jp/english.html

Can I join? No? I bought this drum specially...

Culture show — NTJ has two theatres: Large and Small

Best of the rest
Read all about it

❶
Newsstands, citywide
Mini market

Tokyo's newspaper kiosks are predictably pint-sized. These one-person retail pods go by such names as Metro's and Kiosk and have been a fixture on railway-station platforms for a number of decades.

This is a country where the national dailies and sports tabloids still sell both morning and evening editions so the kiosk racks are constantly having to be restocked. That said, you don't just come here for newspapers: think of these booths as miniature convenience stores that are spilling over with drinks, chocolate, snacks, souvenirs and tissues.

An added bonus is that because you can purchase anything that takes your fancy with a commuter card, you're less likely to miss your train while fumbling for change. You will find kiosks on the platforms or outside turnstiles at many of the largest train and subway stations around the city.

Perfect rhythm

If you want to hear the best J-pop acts, turn on the radio. Broadcasters haven't changed their round-the-clock diet of music, news and interviews for decades.
01 Tokyo FM, 80.0 FM
02 J-Wave, 81.3 FM
03 Inter FM, 76.1 FM

②
Magazines, citywide
Vital signs

Anyone looking for proof that print is not dead should visit Tokyo. Consider the number of Japanese magazine titles in circulation: 3,179 at last count. In 2014, publishers sold 2.6 billion magazine copies and sales topped ¥850bn; staggering figures given the rise of online media. It's a rich market where the micro-demographic is king. Just when you think every niche has been targeted, along comes another publication that takes things a step further.

Many of our favourite titles originate from a single publisher, Magazine House, which is based in Higashi-Ginza. ❶ *Brutus* is for fans of design, fashion and dining with a sprinkling of the latest film, book and music releases. For those fashion-conscious young men who care about keeping up with the latest clothes, culture and food there is the recently revamped ❷ *Popeye* ("Magazine for City Boys"). ❸ *& Premium* is a new

addition to the magazine market for women who want to break out of the standard age/style/hobby categories. Organic-food-loving female readers will find plenty of bento-box recipes and features about homeware in the pages of ❹ *Kunel* while ❺ *Casa Brutus* extends its sister title *Brutus*'s lifestyle coverage to include interiors and architecture. Among English-language publications available in Tokyo, *The Japan Times* and *The Japan News by The Yomiuri Shimbun* carry daily news, while the ❻ *Nikkei Asian Review* offers a weekly wrap-up of political and business news (full disclosure: Nikkei is a MONOCLE investor).

❻
The Nikkei Asian Review is a popular weekly

Design and architecture
—— A tale of two cities

History has been hard on Tokyo's architecture: fire, earthquakes, bombs and high-speed economic development have all left their mark on this sprawling, enthralling capital.

The architectural scene is as dynamic as it is unsentimental but some buildings have managed to survive; the sense of history is barely hidden by the city's superficial modernity. The Tokyo Olympics in 1964 were a key moment for Japanese architecture and many of its monuments remain.

With the bombast of the bubble years in the past, architecture is more thoughtful these days. Where once the red-brick station would have been razed and redeveloped, it was recently given a top-to-toe makeover.

Design comes naturally to Japan, a country where a graphic heritage of family crests has progressed to brand design. Function is the driving force, from the brilliantly complex wrapping of a shop-bought rice ball to an underground bike-parking system that works like a dream.

①
Tokyo Central Post Office, Marunouchi
Rescued rarity

Modern architecture has few champions in Tokyo so it came as a surprise when the then-communications minister Kunio Hatoyama rushed to the defence of the city's striking Central Post Office in 2009. Completed in 1931, the elegant, airy building – one of the only prewar survivors of its kind in central Tokyo – was due to be replaced with a more profitable skyscraper. Hatoyama's intervention brought about a rare reprieve, which saved the façade. It still functions as originally intended but now fronts a 38-storey tower, which houses the headquarters of Japan Post and the Kitte shopping centre.
2-7-2 Marunouchi, Chiyoda-ku
+81 (0)3 3217 5231
jptower.jp

Jiyu Gakuen Myonichikan, Ikebukuro
Wright stuff restored

After Frank Lloyd Wright's Imperial Hotel was demolished in 1968, fans of the architect's work put up a fight to save his Jiyu Gakuen Myonichikan. Known as "House of Tomorrow", the Ikebukuro complex was built for a girls' school in 1921 during Wright's sojourn in Japan. The buildings fell into a sad state of disrepair but were extensively renovated for the site's reopening in 2001. When there are no events being held visitors are welcome to take a look around for a small entrance fee.
2-31-3 Nishi Ikebukuro, Toshima-ku
+81 (0)3 3971 7535
jiyu.jp

Kyu Maeda House, Komaba
Titled grandeur

Komaba Park would be worth visiting if you were just looking to throw down a blanket and sit in the sun but it's also the location of the former home of Marquis Toshinari Maeda. Construction began on the brick mansion in 1929, to the European-style design of architects Yasushi Tsukamoto and Teitaro Takahashi. The decor blends Italian marble, French silk, English furniture and Japanese motifs.

Maeda, an army general, was killed in 1942 and his house was used by the US occupation until the the city took it over in 1964. Closed Mondays and Tuesdays.
4-3-55 Komaba, Meguro-ku
+81 (0)3 3466 5150

Modernism
Boom builds

① Tokyo Bunka Kaikan, Ueno
Sound structure

This concert hall in Ueno Park was designed by Kunio Maekawa and opened in 1961 to celebrate Tokyo's 500th anniversary. The concrete structure is striking but the interior is also remarkable, not least for the wooden reliefs by sculptor Ryokichi Muka on either side of the main stage: looks aside, their design improves the sound. The Main Hall holds 2,300 people, the Recital Hall has room for 650 and there is a music library and rehearsal room. It was refurbished from 1997 to 1999 but admirers hope talk of redevelopment comes to nothing.
5-45 Ueno-Park, Taito-ku
+81 (0)3 3828 2111
t-bunka.jp/en

② Nakagin Capsule Tower, Shimbashi
Catch it while you can

He became one of the best-known architects in Japan but Kisho Kurokawa's finest hour was this apartment block. A product of his metabolist-movement period, it was the world's first capsule structure; it was built in 1972, when ideas for high-density urban living still had a sci-fi quality. Its 140 capsules stack up to a 13-storey tower.

The idea was that units could be built off-site, complete with furniture and appliances, hoisted onto the building and attached to a concrete core. In spite of its architectural fame, Nakagin is utterly neglected and rumours of redevelopment swirl.
8-16-10 Ginza, Chuo-ku

Transient beauty

One of Kisho Kurokawa's last buildings was the vast National Art Centre in Roppongi. Notable for its curved glass façade, this 'empty museum' hosts temporary art exhibitions. The design shop, Souvenir from Tokyo, sells Japanese products.
nact.jp

③
International House of Japan,
Roppongi
Modernist marvel

"I-House", which has offered
visiting writers and academics
somewhere to sleep, work and eat
since the 1950s, is a highlight of
postwar Japanese modernism.

The main building is from 1955,
designed by an architectural dream
team of Kunio Maekawa, Junzo
Sakakura and Junzo Yoshimura.
An annexe (based on Maekawa's
design) was added in 1976.

A stunning Japanese garden,
designed by legendary seventh-
generation Kyoto gardener Jihei
Ogawa, provides the backdrop.
A team from Kyoto still visits to
prune and groom it to perfection.
The house is for members only
but visitors can enjoy the garden
from the Sakura Restaurant or the
Tea Lounge. Note the Lounge's
Persimmon chairs by Daisaku
Choh, another genius of mid-
century Japanese design.
5-11-16 Roppongi, Minato-ku
+81 (0)3 3470 4611
i-house.or.jp

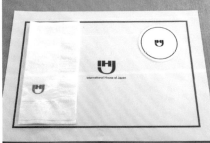

④
St Mary's Cathedral, Sekiguchi
Old master's icon

Prolific architect Kenzo Tange's
concrete St Mary's Cathedral was
built in 1964 to replace the original
Catholic church on the site that was
destroyed during the war. From the
ground, Tange's design recalls a bird
with outstretched wings soaring
upward to the heavens.
3-16-15 Sekiguchi, Bunkyo-ku
+81 (0)3 3945 0126
cathedral-sekiguchi.jp

City visionary
—
Look out
for more of
Tange's work
in Tokyo

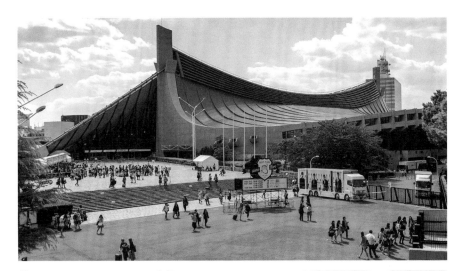

⑤

Yoyogi National Gymnasium,
Harajuku
Winning venue

The 1964 Tokyo Olympics gave the
city some memorable landmarks
but this complex by the late Kenzo
Tange is the best of the lot. The
swooping roof of the larger arena is
an exhilarating sight, recalling both
a shrine and an upturned boat.

Designed for swimming and
diving events, today the arena – now
without the main swimming pool
– is a venue for music and sport.
It is the standard to which others
are held, including Zaha Hadid's
controversial National Stadium,
due to be completed by 2019.
2-1-1 Jinnan, Shibuya-ku
+81 (0)3 3468 1171
jpnsport.go.jp/yoyogi

⑥

Nippon Budokan, Kudanshita
Martial law

Another remnant of the 1964
Tokyo Olympics, the Nippon
Budokan was built as a martial-
arts hall by Mamoru Yamada,
one of the original pioneers of
Japanese modernism in the 1920s.
The architectural reference was
highbrow: the octagonal *Yumedono*
(Hall of Dreams) from Horyu-ji
temple in Nara, with a touch of
Mount Fuji in the slope of the roof.
The Budokan is still primarily a
martial-arts arena but it has also
been used as a music venue since
The Beatles played here, somewhat
controversially, in 1966.
2-3 Kitanomaru Koen, Chiyoda-ku
+81 (0)3 3216 5100
nipponbudokan.or.jp

In the area

01 **National Museum of
Modern Art, Tokyo,
Kudanshita:** The Nippon
Budokan (*see left*) is in
Kitanomaru Park, which
is also the location for
the National Museum
of Modern Art by
Yoshiro Taniguchi.

02 **Kogeikan Crafts Gallery,
Kudanshita:** You can
also visit this, the nearby
museum annexe, for
Japanese craft exhibitions.
Housed in a redbrick
building from 1910.
momat.go.jp

Lap of luxury
—
Walk towards Harajuku from
the Gymnasium, pass over
the bridge (noting the sporting
reliefs) and you'll come to
Co-op Olympia, which was
built just after the Olympics in
1965 and was one of Tokyo's
first luxury apartment blocks,
known in Japanese as
a 'manshon'.

**Contemporary architecture:
Prada Aoyama, Aoyama**

From its rhomboid shape to
its transparent façade, clad
top to bottom in glass panels,
the Prada store immediately
announced itself as a step
forward for retail architecture.
Designed by Swiss duo Herzog
& de Meuron, it opened in
2003 just as all the luxury
labels were building landmarks
around the city. This one has
stood the test of time, glowing
at night like an *andon* lantern.
*5-2-6 Minami Aoyama,
Minato-ku*
+81 (0)3 6418 0400
prada.com

⑦
Reiyukai Shakaden, Azabudai
Imposing presence

This hulking temple, completed in
1975 for the Reiyukai Buddhist sect
– a lay movement founded in 1930
– rises from the cramped streets
of Azabudai. The roof is a feat of
engineering and is best viewed from
the nearby Tokyo Tower, which
offers a good bird's-eye view of the
city. The temple complex is known
as the Shakaden and functions as
a meeting place and social centre.
Takenaka Corporation takes design
credit for the temple, which has
six underground floors and three
above. For other modern temple
architecture, it's worth looking
at Kengo Kuma's much quieter
Baisou-in in Gaienmae.
1-7-8 Azabudai, Minato-ku

While you're here
──

Other landmarks near Reiyukai
Shakaden include Tokyo
Tower (the broadcast tower
whose function has now
been taken by the 634-metre-
tall Skytree), Zojoji Temple
and Atago Jinja, an old
Shinto shrine famous for its
particularly steep staircase.

Traditional architecture
Roots of style

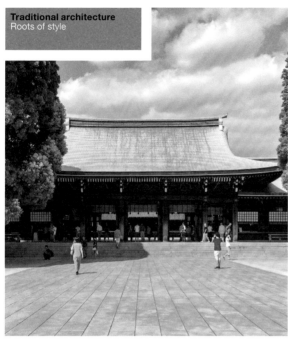

②
Kyu Asakura House, Daikanyama
Taisho-era survivor

An unexpected find in the middle of Daikanyama and just five minutes from the station, this house was built in 1919 as the home of Torajiro Asakura, the head of Tokyo's Prefectural Assembly. That it survived the 1923 earthquake is remarkable enough; that developers never got their hands on it even more so.

The main part of the house is built in a traditional style with a wood-and-plaster exterior and clay tiles on the roof. Inside are *tatami* mats, sliding doors and a *yoma* (western-style room) for visitors.

The *suginoma* (cedar rooms) overlooking the beautifully manicured Japanese garden are a world away from the fashionable boutiques and restaurants outside. Taisho-era buildings are rare in Tokyo and this tranquil piece of the city's history is worth savouring.
29-20 Sarugaku-cho, Shibuya-ku
+81 (0)3 3476 1021

①
Meiji Shrine, Harajuku
Japanese spirit

For anyone with limited time and no plans that extend beyond Tokyo, a quick trip to the Shinto shrine dedicated to Emperor Meiji reveals important lessons about Japanese design. The Meiji era ended in 1912 and, like most of Tokyo, the shrine was flattened by wartime bombing. The rebuild from 1958 is authentic and a reminder of the influence of traditional architectural forms on modern Japanese aesthetics.

Simplicity and space are key although you will have to arrive first thing for a sense of peace: crowds flock here all year round and if you visit on a regular weekend you're likely to see a Shinto wedding party. The shrine's luminous copper roof, nestled in a forest that dates back nearly 100 years, is visible from skyscrapers all over Tokyo.
1-1 Yoyogi Kamizono-cho,
Shibuya-ku
+81 (0)3 3379 5511
meijijingu.or.jp

I've built my own shrine.
No, really! Come see...

①
Tokyo Metropolitan Teien Art
Museum, Meguro
Grand design

This museum occupies the grounds
of the 1930s home of Prince Yasuhiko
Asaka and his wife Princess Nobuko.
It was designed by a team that
included the French glass designer
René Lalique. After three years of
renovation the house was reopened
in 2014 with a new minimalist annexe
(*pictured, bottom left*) designed by
photographer Hiroshi Sugimoto.
5-21-9 Shirokanedai, Minato-ku
+81 (0)3 3443 0201
teien-art-museum.ne.jp

②
Edo-Tokyo Open Air Architectural
Museum, Koganei
Outdoor pursuits

This outdoor annexe to the Edo-
Tokyo Museum is an architectural
park on the outskirts of the city.
Home to buildings from a Tokyo
that has long since disappeared, it
is a revelation. From farmhouses
to public baths, prewar shops and
even a *kabuki* theatre, there are
buildings here that have been saved
from the ravages of earthquakes
and developers. The museum also
has a number of private residences,
including the 1942 home of the
architect Kunio Maekawa.
3-7-1 Sakura-cho, Koganei
(inside Koganei Park)
+81 (0)42 388 3300
tatemonoen.jp

Step back
—
This open-air
museum is
a historical
treat

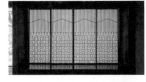

21_21 Design Sight, Roppongi
Underground scene

Fashion designer Issey Miyake
was the driving force behind this
small-scale exhibition space, which
opened in the garden of the Tokyo
Midtown complex in 2007. He
had long called for the city to build
its own design museum but when
public funds weren't forthcoming
he created this unusual venue to
host a roster of playful, thematic
exhibitions featuring the work of
designers from Japan and abroad.
  Miyake remains a director,
alongside two other big names in
Japanese creative business: celebrated
product designer Naoto Fukusawa
and renowned graphic designer Taku
Satoh. The building was designed by
architect Tadao Ando, who covered
the ground level with a low steel roof
and buried the rest of the museum
underground. Fellow architect
Kengo Kuma designed the nearby
Suntory Museum of Art.
9-7-6 Akasaka, Minato-ku
+81 (0)3 3475 2121
2121designsight.jp

GA Gallery, Sendagaya
Expert views

Specialist architecture gallery
and bookshop in Sendagaya
run by the publishers of one of
Japan's best-known architecture
magazines: the bi-monthly *GA* (as
in *Global Architecture*) *Japan*. The
gallery hosts talks by architectural
superstars such as Tadao Ando.
3-12-14 Sendagaya, Shibuya-ku
+81 (0)3 3403 1581
ga-ada.co.jp

Toto Gallery Ma, Nogizaka
Small is beautiful

Toto, Japan's biggest toilet
manufacturer (maker of the famed
Washlet), sponsors this small
architecture-and-design space. It
has punched above its weight for 30
years, showing some of the biggest
names in Japanese architecture.
3F, Toto Nogizaka Building,
1-24-3 Minami Aoyama, Minato-ku
+81 (0)3 3402 1010
toto.co.jp/gallerma

6
Ginza Graphic Gallery, Ginza
Tokyo types

Exhibitions of contemporary
graphics in a gallery run by
venerable Japanese printing
company Dai Nippon Printing.
Exhibitions include work by the
Tokyo Type Directors Club.
1F, DNP Ginza Building,
7-7-2 Ginza, Chuo-ku
+81 (0)3 3571 5206
dnp.co.jp/gallery/ggg_e

①

Rooftops, citywide
Rise above it all

With space at a premium, gardens
are a luxury few can afford in
Tokyo. Look hard though and
you will find the city's rooftops
host plenty of green spaces. Most
department stores have a roof
garden: Marui in Shinjuku has
Q-Court, planted with grass, vines,
roses and clematis, while Isetan's
I-Garden has a lawn and seasonal
flowers. Every summer these and
other rooftop spaces are turned
into beer gardens for alfresco
eating and drinking.

    Property developer Mori
Building, owner of Roppongi Hills
and Ark Hills, has turned many of
its drab roofs into verdant spaces.
Ark Hills has several green spots,
including a secluded roof garden
of fragrant flowers, herbs and
trees. High-rise Roppongi Hills
is covered with rooftop greenery
including a rice paddy, persimmon
trees, ponds and vegetable plots.

    One of the most ambitious
urban greenery projects is at
Ohashi Junction, a towering
highway intersection in Meguro.
The city spent ¥1bn on planting
more than 1,000 trees and shrubs
alongside vegetables and herbs to
create the vertiginous Sky Garden,
which is open to the public daily.

Green peace
——
Tokyo boasts great spaces to escape the bustle

2

Shinjuku Gyoen National Garden, Shinjuku
Hidden treasure

Look at Tokyo from a tall building and you will see three distinct green areas: Yoyogi Park (and adjacent Meiji Shrine), the gardens of the Imperial Palace and Shinjuku Gyoen National Garden.

Where most Tokyo parks function as an extension of people's living rooms and dancing and music practice are standard, Shinjuku Gyoen has a small entry fee and strict rules, with no alcohol and no ball games among them.

It was built on the site of a feudal lord's residence, set over 600 sq m, and became an Imperial garden in 1906. Opened to the public in 1949, today it includes a formal French garden, a Japanese garden and a greenhouse. In spring the sight of its 1,100 cherry trees in bloom is one of the best Tokyo has to offer.
11 Naito-cho, Shinjuku-ku
+81 (0)3 3350 0151
env.go.jp/garden/shinjukugyoen

Four more

01 **Rikugien Gardens, Honkomagome:** Classic 300-year-old Japanese garden that replicates 88 scenes of poetry.
6-16-3 Honkomagome, Bunkyo-ku
+81 (0)3 3941 2222

02 **Koishikawa Korakuen, Korakuen:** 17th-century Chinese-influenced garden.
1-6-6 Koraku, Bunkyo-ku
+81 (0)3 3811 3015

03 **Hamarikyu Teien, Hamarikyu:** Former duck-hunting ground with a traditional tea house.
1-1 Hamarikyu Teien, Chuo-ku
+81 (0)3 3541 0200

04 **Kiyosumi Gardens, Kiyosumi:** 19th-century stroll garden.
3-3-9 Kiyosumi, Koto-ku
+81 (0)3 3641 5892

Delivery services' branding
Streets ahead

You can't miss them in Tokyo: the army of deliverymen and women who race around on scooters, in vans and on foot. This is a city of convenience where people send anything and everything (even chilled food and drink, using cooled vehicles) via a cheap and easy delivery system known as *takkyubin*. Each company has its distinctive uniform and logo: the oldest, Yamato (since 1919), has its famous *kuroneko* (black cat) carrying a kitten in its mouth; there is the blue-and-white stripe of Sagawa Express; and Ecohai, the eco-friendly bicycle-based delivery firm, has a bright green livery.

②
Metro-manners posters
Picture of politeness

Since 1974, Tokyo Metro has produced posters encouraging passengers to behave nicely towards each other. Every year there is a different design and each month a new poster. Sometimes these posters are bilingual but even for Japanese the pictures tell the story. Most convey what other travellers are likely to be thinking: "Don't you realise? The sound is leaking from your headphones," or, "When you cough, please cover your mouth," and, "Why do you ignore those waiting and push in line?" A reminder of the importance of good manners, particularly on busy trains.

Vending machines
Always open

Vending machines (*jihanki*) are a feature of every street and station platform in Tokyo, selling everything from cigarettes and newspapers to ice cream, beer, coffee and snacks. There are more than five million around Japan running 24/7. Drinks companies vie with each other to produce hit beverages and machines offer hot or cold drinks depending on the season.

The earthquake in 2011 and subsequent shutdown of Japan's nuclear reactors prompted *jihanki* manufacturers to work on a new generation of energy-saving drinks dispensers. Coca-Cola Japan collaborated with Fuji Electric on a "peak-shift" vending machine that revs up at night to chill drinks when demand is low and keeps them cold – without power – for up to 16 hours. The new machine uses 95 per cent less electricity during the day than a conventional one.

You don't even need change to use most machines: a tap of your travel pass will do. The best looking of all the *jihanki* is JR East Water Business's Acure touch-screen vending machine: it pops up in stations all over Tokyo.

Manhole covers

In an age when most pedestrians' eyes are locked on their phones, who pays attention to what's happening on the ground? Good urban design is everywhere, even at your feet. Look down and you'll see cast-iron manhole covers everywhere. Many organisations have them, including Tokyo Gas, the police, the Bureau of Waterworks and NTT (Nippon Telegraph and Telephone). Tokyo's sewage bureau alone is in charge of 480,000.

The most common design is a cherry blossom with a gingko leaf and a seagull. Occasionally a more colourful one turns up, the product of a municipal fad for cheering up the lowly manhole. Most are made outside Tokyo by Hinode in Fukuoka or Nagashima Imono in Saitama. Discussions are underway for a special manhole design for the 2020 Olympics.

Transport architecture
Motion slickness

Spin cycle
—
Smart pods
hide space
for 800 bikes
below

① Bike parking
Wheel solutions

It's all very well encouraging people to get on their bikes but what do you do in crowded cities where space is in short supply and street-parking is not allowed? Giken, an engineering company in the city of Kochi, has come up with the ingenious Eco Cycle: a multistorey underground "car park" for bikes. Bicycles are automatically drawn into a small lift and moved down into a parking slot, where they remain hidden from view.

Pavement clutter is banished in an instant and bicycles are securely stored away. Retrieval is simple: a quick swipe of a smart card and within seconds your bike pops out again at ground level.

② Coin locker
Stash and go

Rushing around the city with heavy shopping, laptop and gym kit can be a burden but, as with everything else in Tokyo, if you have a problem someone has the solution. In this case every station has a wall of lockers where, for a few hundred yen, you can safely leave your baggage. For many you don't even need coins: a Pasmo or Suica travel pass can be used as payment.

*Seriously?
Have you
seen me try
to ride a
bike?*

Sport and fitness
—— Be active

Swimming pools
Make a splash

Making waves
Both indoor and outdoor swimming are an option

東京体育館
TOKYO METROPOLITAN GYMNASIUM

With an abundance of parks and riverside walkways, Tokyo offers plenty for visitors who want to stay healthy and fit during a short stay. In this section you will find ideas for a stroll, run or massage while you're exploring the city. There is a wealth of swimming pools, bathhouses and skating rinks, plus the city is dotted with sculpted gardens and temple grounds that are perfect for escaping the noise or meditating.

Though Tokyo is a cinch to get around by train and on foot, we suggest taking to the streets on a bike. And once you've finished your workout we have listings for a haircut, pedicure and shave that will have you looking your best.

Tokyo Metropolitan Gymnasium, Sendagaya
Spoilt for choice

This newly renovated indoor pool complex has extensive gym facilities run by the fitness chain Tipness. Make use of the athletics track, futsal court and fitness studio, as well as the 50-metre and 25-metre pools. Tattoos allowed.
1-17-1 Sendagaya, Shibuya-ku
+81 (0)3 5474 2114
tef.or.jp/tmg/en_index.jsp

②
Aqua Field Pool, Shiba Koen
Convenient complex

Close to Tokyo Tower and Zojoji temple is this modern sports complex with a 50-metre outdoor pool plus a play pool for children. The pools are open from July to mid-September; the rest of the year they become futsal courts.
2-7-2 Shiba Koen, Minato-ku
+81 (0)3 5733 0575
minatoku-sports.com/facilities/aqua

Meguro Citizens' Centre Pool, Meguro
Well-kept waters

This 50-metre outdoor pool has a separate splash pool for toddlers and a wide deck. Open from July to early September but there is also a year-round indoor pool. Strict policy of no tattoos or jewellery.
2-4-36 Meguro, Meguro-ku
+81 (0)3 3711 1139
city.meguro.tokyo.jp/shisetsu/
shisetsu/kumin_center

Bathing in a sento

A soak in the neighbourhood *sento*, or public bathhouse, was once a daily ritual for the city's residents. These days they mainly attract retirees who know what it's like to have lived without bathtubs. In Tokyo the number has been declining for years but several hundred are still in business and charge a low fee set by local authorities. The traditional decor is a large mural of Mount Fuji, though in recent years a handful of new bathhouses and hot-spring theme parks with saunas and mineral baths have emerged to offer a modern take. Before you go, familiarise yourself with the etiquette: remove your shoes at the entrance, strip in the locker room and scrub yourself clean sitting on a stool at one of the very low showers beforehand.

Bathhouses:

01 Tsurunoyu, Sendagaya:
*4-16-4 Sendagaya,
Shibuya-ku*

02 Daikokuyu, Yokokawa:
*3-12-14 Yokokawa,
Sumida-ku
daikokuyu.com/english*

03 Atamiyu, Kagurazaka:
*3-6 Kagurazaka,
Shinjuku-ku*

04 Konparuyu, Ginza:
8-7-5 Ginza, Chuo-ku

05 Inariyu, Takinogawa:
*6-27-14 Takinogawa,
Kita-ku*

If I start snoring will they throw me out?

Alternative ways to stay fit
Activities

Fishing
Ichigaya Fishing Centre, Ichigaya

Not many residents go fishing in the city's waterways but here urban anglers can practice their casting. The facility, located on what was once the outer moat of Edo Castle, has five rectangular pools filled with carp. Plastic crates double as chairs and only catch-and-release fishing is allowed. You win points for your haul; collect enough and you get an extra hour for free.
*1-1 Ichigaya-tamachi, Shinjuku-ku
+81 (0)3 3260 1324
ichigaya-fc.com*

Shiatsu massage
*Namikoshi Shiatsu Salon,
Uchisaiwai-cho*

Shiatsu means "finger pressure" and relieves aches and pains. Pioneer Tokujiro Namikoshi's grandson Takashi runs this venue in the Imperial Hotel. Clients include sumo wrestlers.
*4F, Imperial Hotel Plaza, 1-1-1
Uchisaiwai-cho, Chiyoda-ku
+81 (0)3 3581 7354
namikoshi-shiatsu.co.jp*

My beard is weighing me down

Climbing
Miyashita Park, Shibuya

Tokyo has an abundance of indoor climbing walls but the best outdoor walls are in Miyashita Park. There are two – 7.5 metres for rope climbing and 4 metres for bouldering – and equipment rentals are available. Users must have a climbing certificate or take a test.
*6-20-10 Jingumae, Shibuya-ku
fidosports.jp*

Ice skating
Meiji Jingu Gaien, Sendagaya

Where do Japan's Olympic hopefuls perfect their spins? Meiji Jingu Gaien skating rink. The stadium is a popular venue that hosts tournaments and attracts plenty of young figure-skaters practising amid the crowds.
*11-1 Kasumigaoka-machi,
Shinjuku-ku
+81 (0)3 3403 3458
meijijingugaien.jp*

Time for tee
Although central Tokyo has no golf courses, anyone looking to squeeze in a few practice swings can do so at Meiji Jingu Gaien's driving range. Nearby are baseball batting cages and lawn-tennis courts with an all-white dress code.
meijijingugaien.jp

5

Rajio taiso, citywide
In sync and on air

For many Japanese, mornings
wouldn't be the same without *rajio
taiso*: synchronised exercises done
to a piano accompaniment that
are broadcast on radio and TV.
Several times a day, instructors
lead the nation through one of
three routines, the first starting at
06.30. More than eight decades
after Japan's post-office employees
started *rajio taiso* the practice is
still going strong, with roughly one
in five doing the routines. Retirees
do it in parks, children learn it
at school and office and factory
workers start their day with it.
Staying limber is only part of its
appeal; the feeling of belonging to
a group is just as important.

I feel more supple just watching

Pump it in the park
———
If you're up early, join
the 'rajio taiso' groups at
Setagaya Park on Tokyo's
west side or on the lawn
at Kitanomaru Park in the
centre of the city (though
nobody shows up on rainy
days). Many neighbourhood
parks have dedicated
groups, too.

TV workouts
———
NHK General
and NHK
Education air
rajio taiso

Meditation

Zen Buddhism teaches meditation to calm the mind. In Tokyo there are many temples that give novices a chance to experience this. If you go, don't forget to dress comfortably (but no shorts or tank tops), remove jewellery and watches and make sure your mobile phone is turned off. Here are three worth a look.

Temples:

01 Kourin-in, Hiroo: Walk-ins are welcome, there's no charge and there is even an English manual. Hour-long sessions are held on weekdays from 07.00 and on Sundays from 17.00.
kourin-in.com

02 Choukoku-ji, Azabu: The fee is just ¥100 and no appointment is needed at this working monastery. Sessions are held on Mondays from 18.30 to 20.30 but first-time meditators should arrive at least half an hour early to register.
choukokuji.jiin.com

03 Rinsen-ji, Kohinata: There's a suggested donation of ¥500 and sessions are held Wednesdays from 18.30 to 21.00. You need to call to reserve a spot at least a day beforehand and registration closes 10 minutes before sessions. English handouts provided.
+81 (0)3 3943 0605

I'm meditating on where my next biscuit will come from

Haircare and grooming
Post-workout pruning

Cut above
—
The Barber in Shibuya has hi-tech chairs

①
The Barber, Shibuya
Classic cut

Hiro Matsuda opened The Barber in 2006, combining the skills and services of hair salons with the feel of a western-style barbershop (plus hi-tech leather chairs and wash basins on robotic arms). Matsuda, who trained under Vidal Sasoon, has six shops that mainly target men.
22-15 Maruyama-cho, Shibuya-ku
+81 (0)3 5728 6558
thebarber.jp

②
Abbey, Aoyama
Sparkling tresses

This polished salon has two branches in upmarket Aoyama and is staffed by 17 stylists. A head-and-shoulder massage is part of the service and there is an optional hair wash in carbonated water. For extra pampering, ask for the VIP room.
3F, Ruelle Aoyama A, 4-21-26 Minami Aoyama, Minato-ku
+81 (0)3 3405 6655
abbey2007.com

③
Uka, Tokyo Midtown
The upper hand
Ladies (and men) love the manicures and pedicures at Uka, the salon chain founded by star manicurist Kiho Watanabe. The Tokyo Midtown branch overlooks the garden below and the menu extends to hair, face and body treatments and even a "head spa" where therapists revive tired hair. On offer for men: hair care, eyebrow trimming and nail buffing. There is also a café and a product range that features the popular Uka Nail Oil.
2F, Tokyo Midtown Galleria, 9-7-4 Akasaka, Minato-ku
+81 (0)3 5413 7236
uka.co.jp

④
Barber Oikawa, Hibiya
Old-school service

Barber Oikawa, at The Imperial Hotel, has been offering the clean, wet shave for decades. In business since the end of the Second World War (when the hotel was still in the building designed by Frank Lloyd Wright), the shop has old-world trappings – wooden lockers and mini chandeliers on the mirrors – that you rarely find anywhere else.
B1F, The Imperial Hotel Arcade, 1-1-1 Uchisaiwai-cho, Chiyoda-ku
+81 (0)3 3501 0709
imperial-arcade.co.jp

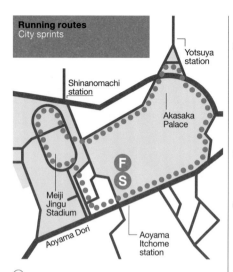

Running routes
City sprints

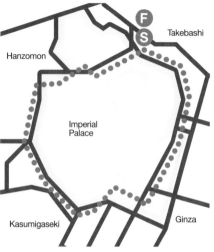

① Togu and Akasaka Palaces
Palatial views

DISTANCE: 4.5km
GRADIENT: Slightly hilly
DIFFICULTY: Medium
HIGHLIGHT: Going past small wooden portals and the main front gates of Akasaka Palace
BEST TIME: Weekends
NEAREST MTR: Aoyama Itchome

This route takes you around the perimeter of Togu and Akasaka palaces and through Meiji Jingu Gaien (Meiji Outer Garden). Few traffic lights will disrupt your rhythm yet you will pass offices, broad boulevards, highways and parks.

Start at the exit from Aoyama Itchome Station and head east along Aoyama Dori for about 1km. Follow the rock wall as it curves left just before Toyokawa Inari Shrine until you come to Sotobori Dori, a road that runs parallel to an elevated section of the Metropolitan Expressway. Turn left and, with the palace wall on your left, head uphill past weather-worn wooden gates and the white gates leading to Akasaka Palace. After this the footpath dips and climbs until you reach the Gondawara intersection. Cross the street and head straight until you are on the loop that takes you around Meiji Jingu Gaien. Past Meiji Jingu Stadium, the city's oldest baseball arena, turn right onto a street lined with gingko trees until, at Aoyama Dori, you turn left to finish your run.

② Imperial Palace loop
High-up lookout

DISTANCE: 5km
GRADIENT: Long incline
DIFFICULTY: Medium
HIGHLIGHT: Running along the moat and past the Sakuradamon Gate
BEST TIME: Mornings
NEAREST MTR: Takebashi, Sakuradamon, Yurakucho, Nijubashimae

This loop, with its uphill stretch and scenic vistas, is a magnet for runners. There's plenty more to like about it: vending machines, public toilets and lots of greenery. Signs along the footpath urge runners to go anti-clockwise, stay on the left unless passing, watch for pedestrians and refrain from littering.

Start at the exit for Takebashi Station, running with the palace moat to your left. The path takes you uphill, past the National Museum of Modern Art and Inuimon Gate (an entrance to the palace's East Gardens, which are off-limits to runners). After veering left you head downhill, curving along the landscaped Sakurada Moat, before a zigzag through Sakuradamon Gate, which was rebuilt based on the original 17th-century design following the Great Kanto Earthquake. Along the last stretch you will see sculpted trees and the downtown office towers. Long-distance runners usually do two or more laps.

Where to buy

Our top spots for running gear: Descente (*descente.jp*) in Harajuku, Gyakusou (*undercoverism.com*) in Aoyama and Asics (*asics.co.jp*) in Ginza.

Running clubs

On Tuesdays the En Route shop in Ginza has a running club from 19.30. Every Wednesday evening, Athletics Far East organises a run from Ikejiri-Ohashi Station.

Locker rooms

Need a changing room for a trot around the Imperial Palace or Yoyogi Park? Head to the city's "running stations". These locker rooms with showers – run by sportswear brands and gym operators – have been popping up all over Tokyo as running has gained popularity.

Running stations:
01 Adidas, Hirakawa-cho:
   adidas.jp/running/runbase
02 Nohara by Mizuno, Harajuku:
   noharabymizuno.jp

Cycling route
Town on two wheels

①
East Tokyo
Waterside ride

An excellent way of getting around Tokyo's old east-side neighbourhoods is by bicycle. But stay vigilant: bike lanes are rare and streets are narrow.

Start with a rental at ❶ *Tokyo Bike* in Yanaka and then head southeast through Ueno Park and past the temples in Asakusa. Continue south along the footpaths of one of the city's main waterways, Sumida River. Stop for a Japanese-style lunch in Kuramae, at ❷*Yuwaeru*. Continue south along the Sumida River until it intersects the Kanda River, where you will find❸*Anatomica*, a fashion retailer.

Head southwest to Bakurocho for the ❹*Röntgenwerke* and ❺ *Cashi* art galleries. Not too far away is ❻ *Starnet*, a shop that specialises in pottery and crafts from the town of Mashiko.

Cross to the east bank of the Sumida River for a walk around ❼*Kiyosumi Garden*, a medieval-period lord's residence. Head back to the west bank of the river to Ningyocho for a *sukiyaki* dinner at ❽*Ningyocho Imahan*.

MONOCLE COMMENT:
Besides Tokyo Bike in Yanaka, other places that are great for bike rentals include Muji at 3-8-3 Marunouchi in Chiyoda-ku (*muji.net*) and Shibuya's Wism at 5-17-20 Jingumae (*wism-tyo.jp*).

Address book

01 **Tokyo Bike**
   4-2-39 Yanaka, Taito-ku
   +81 (0)3 5809 0980
   tokyobike.com
02 **Kuramae**
   2-14-14 Kuramae, Taito-ku
   +81 (0)3 5829 9929
   yuwaeru.co.jp
03 **Anatomica**
   2-27-19 Higashi Nihonbashi, Chuo-ku
   +81 (0)3 5823 6186
   anatomica.jp
04 **Röntgenwerke**
   2-5-17 Nihonbashi Bakuro-cho, Chuo-ku
   +81 (0)3 3662 2666
   roentgenwerke.com
05 **Cashi**
   2-5-18 Nihonbashi Bakuro-cho, Chuo-ku
   +81 (0)3 5825 4703
   cashi.jp
06 **Starnet**
   1-3-9 Higashi-kanda, Chiyoda-ku
   +81 (0)3 5809 3336
   starnet-bkds.com
07 **Kiyosumi Gardens**
   3-3-9 Kiyosumi, Koto-ku
   +81 (0)3 3641 5892
   teien.tokyo-park.or.jp
08 **Ningyocho Imahan**
   2-9-12 Nihonbashi Ningyo-cho, Chuo-ku
   +81 (0)3 3666 7006
   imahan.com

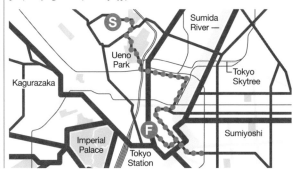

Walks
—— Find your
own Tokyo

Tokyo's numerous
neighbourhoods cover
all walks of life, with
opulent residential
zones, business centres
and edgy upcoming
districts all weaving
into one another. With
construction in Tokyo
as active as ever, the
cityscape is constantly
changing. But here are
five city strolls that best
showcase what the
capital has to offer.

NEIGHBOURHOOD 01
Daikanyama
Upmarket inspiration

Wedged between Shibuya, Ebisu and Naka-meguro,
Daikanyama is a smart neighbourhood of expensive houses,
embassies and small streets dotted with boutiques. Its harsher
edges have been smoothed in recent years – the atmospheric
Dojunkai Apartments, built after the 1923 earthquake, were
demolished to make way for the Daikanyama Address building
– and it is now a magnet for weekenders looking for somewhere
to browse, window shop and enjoy a coffee.

If it's history you're after, take a peek at lovely Kyu Asakura
House, a once-private home from 1919 that has survived both
natural disasters and a World War. Now a museum, the house's
quiet *tatami* rooms and garden, planted with azaleas and maples,
offer respite from the bustle outside.

The heart of Daikanyama has long been Hillside Terrace,
the lifework of one of Japan's great modernist architects,
Fumihiko Maki. He has worked on this unique development,
which includes the Danish Embassy, since 1969. Since 2011
there has been a new focal point: T-Site, a hugely successful
small development that includes the popular book-and-music
shop Tsutaya. Other tenants, such as a dog-grooming salon and
a shop selling designer *mama-chari* (bicycles with kids' seats),
say much about Daikanyama's well-heeled demographic.

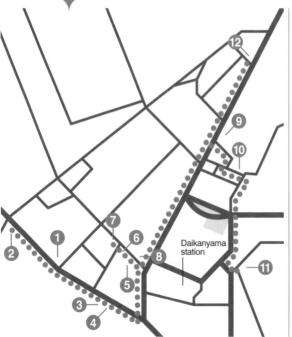

Impeccable taste
Daikanyama walk

Start the walk with an inspiring
hour at ❶ *Tsutaya* bookshop.
Browse the Tokyo travel section
and come away brimming with
ideas. Open from 07.00, it is a
perfect destination for jet-lagged
travellers. Cross the road and stroll
along to ❷ *Saturdays Surf NYC* for
coffee and, on a sunny day, a seat
on its wood-decked terrace, along
the way passing the perennial
favourite eating, drinking and

Daikanyama
station

Getting there
——
Daikanyama is walking
distance from both Ebisu
and Shibuya stations but the
neighbourhood is also served
by its own station on the
Tokyu Toyoko line. It's just
one stop from Shibuya.

Address book

01 **Tsutaya Books**
17-5 Sarugaku-cho,
Shibuya-ku
+81 (0)3 3770 2525
*real.tsite.jp/daikanyama/
english/*

02 **Saturdays Surf NYC**
1-5-2 Aobadai, Meguro-ku
+81 (0)3 5459 5033
saturdaysnyc.com

03 **Tom's Sandwich**
29-10 Sarugaku-cho,
Shibuya-ku
tom-s.com

04 **Greeniche Daikanyama**
29-10 Sarugaku-cho,
Shibuya-ku
greeniche.co.jp

05 **Bonjour Records**
24-1 Sarugaku-cho,
Shibuya-ku
+81 (0)3 5458 6020
bonjour.jp

06 **APC Homme**
25-2 Sarugaku-cho,
Shibuya-ku
+81 (0)3 3496 7570
ww1.apcjp.com/jpn

07 **B-jirushi Yoshida**
19-6 Sarugaku-cho,
Shibuya-ku
+81 (0)3 5428 5951
bjirushi.com

08 **Kamawanu**
23-1 Sarugaku-cho,
Shibuya-ku
+81 (0)3 3780 0182
kamawanu.co.jp

09 **Ogawaken**
10-13 Daikanyama-cho,
Shibuya-ku
+81 (0)3 3463 3809
daikanyama-ogawaken.com

10 **Ao**
10-4 Daikanyama-cho,
Shibuya-ku
ao-daikanyama.com

11 **Cocca**
1-31-13 Ebisu Nishi,
Shibuya-ku
+81 (0)3 3463 7681
cocca.ne.jp

12 **Āta**
1F, 2-5 Sarugaku-cho,
Shibuya-ku
+81 (0)3 6809 0965
ata1789.com

people-watching spot Caffè
Michelangelo (open from 11.00).

Refreshed, retrace your steps
to admire Fumihiko Maki's work
on Hillside Terrace and grab a
ham-and-Swiss-cheese sandwich
at ❸ *Tom's Sandwich*. Peer in at
❹ *Greeniche*, which sells vintage
Scandinavian furniture and new
pieces with equal enthusiasm.

Cross over to the Cordon Bleu
school and then walk around the
corner. Keep on and turn left
towards ❺ *Bonjour Records* for a
tightly edited music selection and
goods from fashion label Kitsuné.
Keep going for menswear shop
❻ *APC Homme*, which has always
found its natural home in Tokyo.
Take the next left and on the
corner is ❼ *B-jirushi Yoshida*, a
collaboration store by Beams and
Tokyo bag-maker Yoshida Kaban.

As well as selling its own products,
brands including MONOCLE, White
Mountaineering and Margaret
Howell are also on offer and a
monogramming service is available
on some lines.

Just behind is Kodomo Beams;
stop by for children's clothes and
accessories from home and abroad,
including cheerfully coloured
wellington boots and rucksacks.
Daikanyama has become a magnet
for upmarket children's clothes;
alongside the grown-up fashion
stores on Kyu-Yamate Dori (*Dori*

meaning "Street") you'll find kids'
brands such as Bonton, Bonpoint
and Caramel Baby & Child.

Cross over the road and walk
back to Hachiman Dori, taking a
left at the corner. Make another
quick left before stopping in at
❽ *Kamawanu* for brightly printed
tenugui cotton cloths.

Head back to the main road
again and turn left, passing APC
Femme then Zucca (the label
started by ex-Issey Miyake
designer Akira Onozuka) and
Tokyo label Tsumori Chisato's
shop. If lunch is calling, walk
on and cross the road for classic
yoshoku (western-style Japanese)
food at ❾ *Ogawaken*, which has
been in business since 1905. The
pace is stately and the waiters are
formally attired. If you pass on
a table, at least buy a tin of the
Raisin Wich biscuits in the
adjacent patisserie.

A brief stroll in the direction you
came lies the Daikanyama Address
tower. Duck behind it to explore
shops such as ❿ *Ao*, a clothes
brand for men, women and
children with its own factory
in Niigata prefecture that
specialises in loose, soft cotton.
Local textile-maker ⓫ *Cocca* sells its
own fabrics and collaborations with
the likes of Tokyo brand Syuro and
textile designer Masafumi Arita. It
also holds workshops where you
can make your own scarves.

Round off your walk with a
coffee at the Motoya Express van
in front of Daikanyama Station or,
if you've worked up more of an
appetite, head back up Hachiman
Dori to ⓬ *Āta* for a seat at the
counter while chef Satoshi
Kakegawa cooks up steak and fries.

NEIGHBOURHOOD 02
Marunouchi
Get down to business

Marunouchi is as close to a central business district as this city has. It's only a few blocks wide, sandwiched between the Imperial Palace moat and the historic Tokyo Station, the city's third-busiest railway depot. But its north-south axis is the middle section of an office district stretching from Yurakucho to Otemachi that private developers and the city have been building skyward since height limits were eased after 2000. The main artery connecting these areas is Naka-Dori, the tree-lined, cobblestoned avenue where global luxury brands and fashion labels have set up shop beside tea salons, Japanese boutiques and restaurants.

Marunouchi was the inlet of a bay until it was filled in during the 16th century, when it became a residential area for feudal lords from out of town. Only after the fall of Japan's last *shogun* in the late 19th century did it begin to take shape as an office district. Over the past two decades Marunouchi has experienced a rebirth: the skyline is higher and more modern, and major global financial, media and consulting players have been steadily moving in.

Much of the credit goes to the area's biggest developer, Mitsubishi Estate, which has created a popular destination for shoppers by setting aside plenty of space for retailers and designing Naka-Dori to be as pedestrian-friendly as possible.

Commercial gain
Marunouchi walk

The Imperial Palace is as good a place as any to start. Five days a week (except Mondays and Fridays), the palace opens its ❶ *East Gardens* for anyone to wander the meandering footpaths and admire the sculpted bushes and flowering plants of one of the city's most fussed-over and tightly guarded public plots. Enter from the Kitahane-bashi-mon gate and cut through the garden, past the Fujimitamon Defence House and the Suwano-chaya Teahouse, to the tile-roofed wooden Ote-mon gate.

Once you exit the palace, head to the ❷ *Aman Tokyo hotel* for a cocktail and extraordinary views of the forested palace grounds and the city's skyline. A few blocks away is the Michael Hopkins-designed ❸ *Shin-Marunouchi Building*, which has more than 150 restaurants and shops and plenty of armchairs and sofas to take the weight off for a bit. Across the street is the ❹ *Marunouchi Building*, a 37-storey tower whose 2002 completion marked the start of a building boom that has transformed Marunouchi into one of the city's most vibrant business and retail areas.

In front of these two towers is the century-old ❺ *Tokyo Station* with more than a dozen local and express trains and Shinkansen (bullet train) lines. The station was recently given a facelift based on early architectural blueprints. Inside there is now a gallery and a 150-room luxury hotel overlooking a dome and a plaza that stretches to the Imperial Palace.

Walk next door to the JP Tower, which opened in 2013 with a façade from the 1931 Tokyo Central Post Office building.

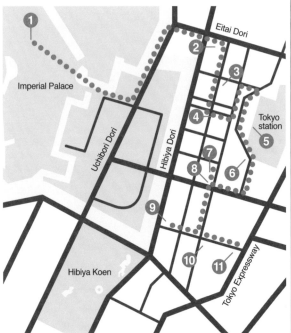

(map)
Imperial Palace
Eitai Dori
Tokyo station
Uchibori Dori
Hibiya Dori
Hibiya Koen
Tokyo Expressway

Inside, ⑥ *Kitte Marunouchi* houses nearly 100 retailers, including Claska Do and Spiral Market, two shops with gifts that mix craftsmanship and modern design. Check out Kitte's sixth-floor terrace overlooking the tracks leading to Tokyo Station.

Then head to Naka-Dori, the 1.2km-long cobblestone street lined with benches, elm trees and hanging flower pots. At lunchtime, when Naka-Dori is closed to traffic, dark-suited workers spill out of the buildings and on weekends events often draw lively crowds. Along this street you'll find Japanese fashion retailers Tomorrowland, Beams, United Arrows' The Sovereign House and Comme des Garçons, along with global brands such as James Perse and Paul Smith.

Before long you will come to Mitsubishi Estate's ⑦ *Marunouchi Brick Square*. Opened in 2009, this leafy plaza and office complex has dozens of restaurants and shops, including Cacao Sampaka from Barcelona, butter specialist Echire from France and Pass the Baton, a modern Japanese vintage

store that sells antiques, art and homeware. Surrounding the square on two sides is the ⑧ *Mitsubishi Ichigokan Museum*, which has a permanent collection of posters, art and books but also shows pieces from a number of global galleries. The building is a faithful recreation of the 1894 Queen Anne-style brick-and-stone office – Marunouchi's first western-style building – that was designed by English architect Josiah Conder but was torn down in 1968. If you're a fan of Broadway musicals, consider catching a show at the ⑨ *Imperial Theatre*. Japanese versions of *Les Misérables*, *Man of La Mancha* and *Miss Saigon* have been staged here. Next, stop by ⑩ *Bic Camera* in front of JR Yurakucho Station. It has one of the city's largest selections of electronics and home appliances, with Japanese brands well represented. End your stroll at the ⑪ *Ginza Sky Lounge*, a revolving restaurant in the Kotsu Kaikan building in Yurakucho, which opened in 1965 and has great views of the bullet trains heading to and from Tokyo Station.

Getting there

Marunouchi is one of the most accessible areas in the city, with more than a dozen JR lines feeding into nearby Tokyo Station. It can also be reached from four Tokyo Metro stations: Marunouchi, Otemachi, Yurakucho and Nijubashimae.

Address book

01 East Gardens, Imperial Palace
1-1 Chiyoda, Chiyoda-ku
+81 (0)3 3213 1111
sankan.kunaicho.go.jp

02 Aman Tokyo
1-5-6 Otemachi, The Otemachi Tower, Chiyoda-ku
+81 (0)3 5224 3333
amanresorts.com

03 Shin-Marunouchi Building
1-5-1 Marunouchi, Chiyoda-ku
+81 (0)3 5218 5100
marunouchi.com

04 Marunouchi Building
2-4-1 Marunouchi, Chiyoda-ku
+81 (0)3 5218 5100
marunouchi.com

05 Tokyo Station
1-9-1 Marunouchi, Chiyoda-ku
tokyostationcity.com/en

06 Kitte Marunouchi
2-7-2 Marunouchi, Chiyoda-ku
+81 (0)3 3216 2811
jptower-kitte.jp

07 Marunouchi Brick Square
2-6 Marunouchi, Chiyoda-ku
+81 (0)3 5218 5100
marunouchi.com

08 Mitsubishi Ichigokan Museum
2-6-2 Marunouchi, Chiyoda-ku
mimt.jp

09 Imperial Theatre
3-1-1 Marunouchi, Chiyoda-ku
toho.co.jp/stage/teigeki

10 Bic Camera
1-11-1 Yurakucho, Chiyoda-ku
+81 (0)3 5221 1112
biccamera.co.jp

11 Ginza Sky Lounge
15F, Kotsu Kaikan Building, 2-10-1 Yurakucho, Chiyoda-ku
+81 (0)3 3212 2776
kaikan.co.jp

NEIGHBOURHOOD 03

Sendagaya
On-the-up creativity

Situated in the centre of Tokyo between Harajuku and Shinjuku, Sendagaya is a neighbourhood dominated by low-rise offices and showrooms for Japanese clothing brands and architecture firms. Lately the once-overlooked area has become a magnet for a close-knit community of retailers and designers who have moved in and set up shop. Sendagaya means "Valley with harvests as big as 1,000 horses could carry", a reference to the fertile rice paddies that once blanketed the area.

The influx of creative businesses began with Shinichiro Nakahara, who moved his design firm Landscape Products and shop Playmountain in 2000. He was drawn to the laidback pace and Sendagaya's proximity to the greenery of Shinjuku Gyoen and Meiji Shrine. He also liked having an address that wasn't known outside the fashion and design world, despite its location in the city centre. Before long his staff had opened a café – Tas Yard – and a coffee kiosk. Nakahara found himself persuading shopkeepers and business owners who shared his devotion to craftsmanship and design to set up a base in the area. With nearby venues set to host the 2020 Tokyo Olympics, Sendagaya could be in for heavier foot traffic in the not too distant future. In the meantime we recommend that you start the trend.

Design circuit
Sendagaya walk

Begin your stroll with a trip to ❶ *GA Gallery*, the editorial office for Global Architecture's magazines that also houses a gallery and bookshop. If you are eager to browse contemporary art, two of the city's most respected galleries – ❷ *Tomio Koyama Gallery* and Taka Ishii Gallery – moved over to Kitasando in mid-2015 from east Tokyo.

For Japanese comfort-food standards of curry rice, hashed beef and sautéed ginger pork, head to ❸ *Tas Yard*. This relaxed café is the creation of Landscape Products and run by Shinichiro Nakahara; it serves as a canteen and informal conference room for many of the designers and fashion types that inhabit the area.

Don't forget to browse the selection of edibles such as dried-fish *dashi* stock from Kagawa prefecture or oil-marinated herring from Kagoshima at Good Neighbors' Fine Foods in a shack attached to the café. From there

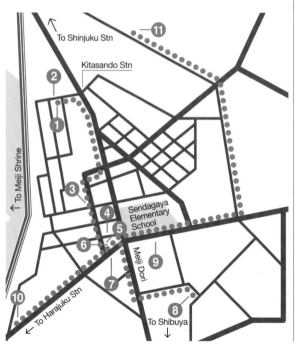

it's a short walk to grab a coffee at the Be A Good Neighbor Coffee Kiosk (motto: "A New Day Starts Here"). The baristas, Yusuke Shinkai and Masahiro Kajihara, have been making espresso and drip-brews since 2010, using beans roasted by Voila Coffee.

If casualwear is on your shopping list, head around the corner to the ❹ *Loopwheeler* shop, where the cult brand founded by Satoshi Suzuki sells sweatshirts, cardigans and T-shirts made on century-old knitting machines.

From there, cross the street to stationery-and-letterpress publisher ❺ *Papier Labo*. The shop is no bigger than a walk-in closet but there are plenty of original items and owner Kimiaki Eto's offbeat wit and sensibility is reflected in every card, notebook and envelope. He also designs and prints business cards on offset-letter printing presses.

On the main street you'll find ❻*Playmountain*, Nakahara's retail space filled with pottery, tableware, toys and knickknacks collected from around Japan and parts of the US. Across the street, ❼ *Tembea* is designer Atsushi Hayasaki's shop specialising in handcrafted bags made out of heavy-duty canvas that are woven in Japan on an old shuttle loom.

For music it's hard to beat Masashi Naka's ❽ *Big Love* record shop, tucked away on the third floor of an apartment complex. Naka's vast collection of LPs, CDs and even old cassette tapes features artists such as Travis Bretzer, American Wrestlers and

Horsebeach. Flip through his vinyl selection and you will find a surprising number of limited-edition albums. In his small café, Naka serves craft-brewer Shiga Kogen's ales on tap alongside other drinks and snacks.

If you want a light meal you have a choice between two great independently run noodle shops of very different styles: ❾ *Pho321 Noodle Bar*, which has Japanese reinterpretations of Vietnamese classics *pho* and *com*, and ramen shop ❿*Afuri*, whose *yuzu* chicken ramen in a clear or creamy soup or *tsukemen* dipping sauce with noodles are guaranteed to have you hooked. Indeed, all that walking might make you hungry enough to try both.

End your tour of Sendagaya with a soak in the hot public bath at ⓫ *Tsuru-no-yu*, a wooden building with a gabled roof and ceramic tiles that belong to a bygone era (open from 15.30 until 23.30). For a small fee, the bath's staff will provide a towel, soap and shampoo.

Getting there

This part of Sendagaya is just off Meiji Dori, which connects Harajuku to Shinjuku and is easy to get to by metro. Take the Fukutoshin line to Kitasando station and walk a few blocks or enjoy a longer stroll to the neighbourhood from JR Harajuku Station.

Address book

01 **GA Gallery**
3-12-14 Sendagaya, Shibuya-ku
+81 (0)3 3403 1581
02 **Tomio Koyama Gallery**
B1F, 3-10-11 Sendagaya, Shibuya-ku
tomiokoyamagallery.com
03 **Tas Yard**
3-3-14 Sendagaya, Shibuya-ku
+81 (0)3 3470 3940
tasyard.com
04 **Loopwheeler**
B1F, 3-51-3 Sendagaya, Shibuya-ku
+81 (0)3 5414 2350
loopwheeler.co.jp
05 **Papier Labo**
3-52-5 Sendagaya, Shibuya-ku
+81 (0)3 5411 1696
papierlabo.com
06 **Playmountain**
3-52-5 Sendagaya, Shibuya-ku
+81 (0)3 5775 6747
playmountain-tokyo.com; landscape-products.net
07 **Tembea**
1-1-12 Jingumae, Shibuya-ku
+81 (0)3 3405 5278
torso-design.com
08 **Big Love**
3F, 2-31-3 Jingumae, Shibuya-ku
+81 (0)3 5775 1315
bigloverecords.jp
09 **Pho321 Noodle Bar**
2-35-9 Jingumae, Shibuya-ku
+81 (0)3 6432 9586
pho321.net
10 **Afuri**
3-63-1 Sendagaya, Shibuya-ku
+81 (0)3 6438 1910
11 **Tsuru-no-yu**
4-16-4 Sendagaya, Shibuya-ku
+81 (0)3 3402 5808

NEIGHBOURHOOD 04
Tomigaya
One of a kind

Fashionable neighbourhoods come and go in Tokyo, morphing from edgy to mainstream in a matter of months. Tomigaya is still on the quirky side: a quiet residential neighbourhood at the back of throbbing Shibuya that is also close to Omotesando and one of the city's largest green spaces: Yoyogi Park.

Still scruffy around the edges, Tomigaya benefits from its proximity to the centre as well as its separation from it. The main artery is the long street known locally as Tokyu Honten Dori, named after the genteel Tokyu Honten department store that sits at the Shibuya end. Go there for the basement food hall and Maruzen & Junkudo bookshop that occupies the entire seventh floor. Honten Dori typifies Tomigaya's mix of old and new: you'll find everything from the local butcher, fishmonger and *tatami* mat-maker to new bookshops, cafés and organic wine bars.

This neighbourhood is also where you will find The Monocle Shop and bureau. Our part of Tomigaya is nestled behind the HQ of the Issey Miyake fashion empire and is close to the home of state broadcaster NHK, from which workers emerge at lunchtime to fill the many small restaurants that populate the neighbourhood. Also nearby is Yoyogi Hachimangu, a lively city shrine with strong links to the local community and an impressive *matsuri* (festival) in September.

Cruise through the bijou
Tomigaya walk

Emerging from Yoyogi Koen station, start with a brisk stroll around Yoyogi Park, one of the city's most popular jogging spots. Also a favourite place for *hanami* cherry-blossom picnics, the park is heaving at weekends with runners, dancing rockabillies and trumpeters who practice outdoors rather than annoy their neighbours at home. Weekday mornings are quiet though and you might be alone save for the odd

pooch in the dog run and groups of nursery children.

Follow your slice of parklife with a coffee at ❶ *Little Nap* just across from the Sangubashi gate. Owner Daisuke Hamada's (*above*) stand is tiny but the queue for his coffee, muffins and brownies is testament to its popularity. For something more substantial stop at ❷ *Mimet* for boiled egg and toast, served until 11.00. Taro Yamamoto has a shop and a couple of other restaurants in the area but Mimet, located in an old house, is his newest venture.

Past Shoichiro Aiba's busy Italian restaurant Life you'll find ❸ *Rhythm and Books*, where Kenji and Eriko Suzuki sell a niche selection of vintage tomes; monographs on mushrooms and illustrated children's books from eastern Europe are a speciality. Cross over the road to Honten Dori, swerving left after FamilyMart to pick up *pastel de nata* custard tarts from the hatch at Nata de Cristiano. This little *doçaria* supplies two nearby Portuguese restaurants of the same name.

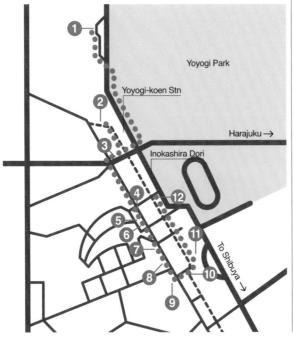

Yoyogi Park

Yoyogi-koen Stn

Harajuku →

Inokashira Dori

To Shibuya →

Back on the main street, pass no-frills Taiwanese restaurant Reikyo. ❹ *The Monocle Shop* is further along the street, next door to ❺ *Pivoine*, which sells an artfully arranged mix of clothes, ceramics and flowers. Miniature schnauzer Stock is usually holding court.

Turn right at the 7-Eleven and take in the food at popular wine bar ❻ *Ahiru Store*, run by brother-and-sister duo Teruhiko and Wakako Saito. Ahiru opens at 18.00 and fills up quickly.

Take a left and up on the right past Camelback café is interior designer Tomoyuki Kamiya's shop ❼ *Archivando*, which sells glass, ceramics, cutlery and stationery. Lunch options abound on this street, including Mongenbo, which serves *kamo nanban* duck soba, and Unagi Yoshino – where owner-chef Yoshino-san has been serving *unagi* (freshwater eel) for nearly three decades.

Another local favourite is ❽ *Uoriki*, a fish shop that is now run by fourth-generation owner Yasuhisa Suzuki. Lunch specials change daily and a sign warns

魚力

Getting there

The nearest metro station is Yoyogi Park on the Chiyoda line but you can also access the neighbourhood from the Shibuya side by walking from Tokyu Honten department store. If you're visiting Meiji Shrine or Harajuku, you could also walk through Yoyogi Park.

profligate diners of a ¥500 penalty for anyone who doesn't finish their rice and miso soup (they hate to see food wasted). Keep walking for a wide selection of reading material at ❾ *Shibuya Publishing Booksellers*. Then, if you're seeking a culture hit, continue towards Shibuya to Uplink cinema or Toguri Museum of Art – otherwise cross the road and walk back, taking the first right turn to find ❿ *Provenance*. Naosuke Hayakawa's shop is a vintage treasure trove, crammed with Scandinavian tableware plus eyewear, toys and furniture.

If you have time for a quick detour stop at ⓫ *Shibuya Cheese Stand* for cheese-maker Shinji Fujikawa's ricotta and mozzarella.

For dinner try Pignon – a bistro run by talented chef Rimpei Yoshikawa on Honten Dori – or Sajiya. Finish things off at ⓬ *Fuglen*, a popular outpost of the Oslo bar that combines coffee, cocktails and vintage Norwegian furniture. At night it serves classics plus original cocktails, including the shiso and ginger-flavoured Oishi-so.

Address book

01 Little Nap
5-65-4 Yoyogi, Shibuya-ku
+81 (0)3 3466 0074
littlenap.jp

02 Mimet
1-7-6 Tomigaya, Shibuya-ku
+81 (0)3 5738 8241
puhura.co.jp

03 Rhythm and Books
1-9-15 Tomigaya, Shibuya-ku
+81 (0)3 6407 0788
rhythm-books.com

04 The Monocle Shop
1-19-2 Tomigaya, Shibuya-ku
+81 (0)3 6407 0845
monocle.com/shop

05 Pivoine
1-19-3 Tomigaya, Shibuya-ku
+81 (0)3 3465 1193
puhura.co.jp

06 Ahiru Store
1-19-4 Tomigaya, Shibuya-ku
+81 (0)3 5454 2146

07 Archivando
41-5 Kamiyama-cho, Shibuya-ku
+81 (0)3 5738 7253
archivando.jp

08 Uoriki
40-4 Kamiyama-cho, Shibuya-ku
+81 (0)3 3467 6709
uoriki6709.com

09 Shibuya Publishing Booksellers
17-3 Kamiyama-cho, Shibuya-ku
+81 (0)3 5465 0588
shibuyabooks.net

10 Provenance
7-15 Kamiyama-cho, Shibuya-ku
+81 (0)3 3469 7633

11 Shibuya Cheese Stand
5-8 Kamiyama-cho, Shibuya-ku
+81 (0)3 6407 9806
cheese-stand.com

12 Fuglen
1-16-11 Tomigaya, Shibuya-ku
+81 (0)3 3481 0884
fuglen.com

NEIGHBOURHOOD 05
Yanaka
Taste of old Tokyo

A few kilometres northeast of Tokyo's fashion and financial districts, near the museums and greenery of Ueno Park, lies Yanaka. One of the few places in Tokyo that was spared in the Allied firebombing raids of the Second World War, Yanaka's lowrise wooden houses with ceramic-tiled roofs give it the small-town feel of prewar Japan. For decades it was a haven for artists and writers, many of whom were affiliated with the fine-arts and music schools (now Tokyo University of the Arts). Yanaka's centuries-old walled temples, meandering streets, traditional architecture and unhurried pace are what make it so charming.

Don't expect the glass-and-steel towers and neon signs that have become the signature look of other parts of Tokyo. The symbolic heart of the district is Yanaka Ginza, a car-free shopping street of sweets sellers, soba restaurants and craft shops that has somehow resisted the invasion of national and global retail chains. Lately Yanaka's low rents, convenient transport links and laidback vibe have attracted a new generation of entrepreneurs. These gallery owners, bakers, restaurateurs and barkeepers have little interest in a fashionable address; they are here for a neighbourhood that has managed to isolate itself from the feverish pace and property-redevelopment rush that have been the norm in postwar Japan.

Easy does it
Yanaka walk

Start your walk at ❶ *Nippori Station*, cutting southwest through Yanaka Cemetery, the final resting place of Japan's last Shogun ruler Yoshinobu Tokugawa. Head west along Dango-zaka to discover Ichiro Kanai's ❷ *Tokyo Bike*, which offers bicycles designed in-house.

A little to the north you'll find the ❸ *Asakura Museum of Sculpture*, former studio and home of Fumio Asakura, a key figure in Japanese art. If the museum has given you a taste for well-crafted artefacts, ❹ *Yanaka Matsunoya* lies just to the west. This branch of the Asakusabashi-based retailer run by third-generation owner Hiroshi Matsuno offers handmade Japanese crafts for everyday use: rice baskets from Sado Island and apple-tree ladders from Aomori.

Head down the steps known as Yuyake Dandan (named after the sunset view that they offer) leading to Yanaka Ginza, a prewar shopping street, and walk south until you reach Dangozaka. To your right you will see ❺ *Kikumi Senbei*, a rice-cracker shop in an old wooden building that opened in 1875 and sells square, hand-grilled crackers. Further along on the left is the even older ❻ *Isetatsu Paper*, which opened in 1864 and is still making its decorative woodblock-printed *chiyogami* paper.

For lunch grab a seat along the counter at ❼ *Lemon-no-Mi*. There's no menu here; the proprietress simply makes one dish a day (sometimes Japanese, often not) that she serves to diners until it's

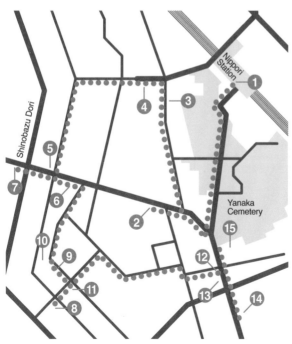

all gone. Another nearby culinary option is **8** *Nezu Takajo*, a popular but hard-to-spot soba restaurant that serves breakfast from 07.30 and lunch until early evening.

For shopping there's no better place than **9** *Classico*. Opened by Ryu Takahashi in 2006, the shop sells antiques, clothes, pottery and crafts. Takahashi's talent is in championing small, mostly Japanese brands that share his belief in making products locally. He now sells own-label Oxford shirts made in Tokyo.

If you ask Takahashi for a recommendation he will doubtless mention **10** *Tabi Bagel* (*tabi* means "travel"), a ground-floor shop in an alleyway known as Hebi-Dori (Snake Street). Here you'll find bagels in three flavours – plain, raisin and a herb, nut and spice *dukka* – along with homemade jams. Takahashi also suggests swinging by Le Coussinet, a patisserie on Aizome-Odori that opens only on Fridays, weekends and holidays to provide chocolate

gateau, custard pudding and other desserts to its loyal customers.

Wander uphill along Aizome-Odori, past **11** *Ryokan Sawanoya*, a Japanese inn, and walled temples until you come to art gallery **12** *Scai the Bathhouse*, run by Masami Shiraishi, a pioneer of Tokyo's contemporary art scene. Shiraishi was behind the effort to reopen the nearby **13** *Kayaba Coffee* (redesigned by architect Yuko Nagayama) in 2009, saving this gem from the wrecking ball. The café which was in business from 1938 until 2006, again serves the crustless sandwiches and other old-fashioned Japanese café favourites for which it was once known.

If you prefer green tea, a block away there's **14** *Torindo*, a *wagashi* Japanese sweetshop with a café that serves *matcha* and sweets, some made on the premises. Shiraishi was also behind the renovation of three 1930s-era wooden homes, collectively called **15** *Ueno Sakuragi Atari*. They house Kayaba Bakery, craft-beer bar Yanaka Beer Hall, condiments shop Oshi Olive and an events space.

Getting there

Yanaka sits conveniently between Sendagi Station on the Tokyo Metro Chiyoda line to the west and JR Yamanote line's Nippori Station to the east. If you want to stretch your legs a bit more, start off at the southern edge of Yanaka from Nezu Station, also on the Chiyoda line.

Address book

Resources
—— Inside knowledge

In Tokyo there is no reason not to use public transport; the rail network extends to almost every corner of the metropolitan area. And once you have witnessed the spotless train cars and attentive staff you will understand why this city of more than 13 million people works so well. Navigating the countless lines and stations with their unfamiliar names can seem daunting but – even when everyone seems to be in a rush – you will encounter people who'll help you figure things out.

Bring your walking shoes and comfortable clothing; you will spend a lot of time outdoors getting around on foot. Tokyo can at times seem impenetrable and overwhelming to anyone who hasn't visited before; there's much to stimulate the senses and the city's sights and smells will take some getting used to. And listen out for words the Japanese have absorbed from other languages and made their own; a few are deciphered for you here.

Transport
Get around town

01 **Commuter cards:** Pasmo and Suica cards work on all railway and bus lines in Tokyo and give you cheaper fares compared to single-ride tickets. Add money to your card at a ticket machine and return it when you leave to get back the ¥500 deposit.
pasmo.co.jp;
jreast.co.jp/suica

02 **Trains:** Tokyo's extensive railway network covers almost every neighbourhood. There are subways, trains, monorails and even a tram. Japan Railway (JR) lines connect to the national Shinkansen high-speed rail network at Tokyo and Shinagawa stations.

03 **Bicycle:** Private rentals run by Muji, Tokyo Bike and Wism are more user-friendly than public schemes. Fees at Muji and Tokyo Bike range from ¥540 to ¥1,080 for the day; Wism charges ¥1,080 for three hours.

04 **Bus:** A scenic but not especially fast way to get around town, city buses are reliably on time but they don't run too frequently. Use your Pasmo or Suica pass or pay the single-ride fare of ¥210.
kotsu.metro.tokyo.jp/eng

05 **On foot:** Tokyo's streets can be a maze: addresses, based on antiquated numbering, are arranged in blocks and streets can lack names. Free wi-fi is hard to come by so rent a portable unit at the airport and use GPS to get around.

06 **Taxi and private car hire:** Taxis start off at ¥730 for the first 2km. If you need to hire a car for the day, ask your hotel concierge to contact taxi operators Nihon Kotsu or KM.
nihon-kotsu.co.jp/en;
km-group.co.jp/en

07 **Flights:** For domestic flights, Haneda is a short trip by monorail or Keikyu line from the city centre. Its retail and food offerings are arguably the best of any airport.
tokyo-airport-bldg.co.jp

Vocabulary
Local lingo

01 **Conbini:** Convenience store
02 **Famiresu:** Family restaurant such as Royal Host
03 **Gochisosama:** Thanks for the meal
04 **Jihanki:** Vending machine
05 **Kaado:** Credit card
06 **Nama:** Draft beer
07 **Okawari:** Second helping of rice
08 **Oomori:** Big portion (food)
09 **Suimasen:** Please/excuse me/sorry
10 **Toire:** Toilet

Soundtrack to the city
Five top tunes

01 **Pizzicato Five, 'Tokyo wa yoru no shichiji':** Known in the West as "The Night is Still Young", this upbeat, ironic pop tune (in Japanese, "It's 7pm in Tokyo") perfectly captures the 1990s Tokyo dance-club scene.

02 **Shizuko Kasagi, 'Tokyo Boogie Woogie':** The Second World War is over, Japan's economy is taking off and the queen of boogie is belting out a tune reflecting the optimism of the era.

03 **Kyu Sakamoto, 'Ue wo muite arukou' (AKA 'Sukiyaki'):** The melody is romantic but this karaoke staple from the early 1960s taps into the frustrations felt after a student demonstration held to protest the postwar US military occupation.

04 **Kyary Pamyu Pamyu, 'Tokyo Highway':** The Harajuku pop princess sings about the fast pace, din and glare of the city. The lyrics could also describe her own musical performances.

05 **Teriyaki Boyz, 'Tokyo Drift':** The all-star cast of rappers and DJs, including A Bathing Ape founder Nigo, composed this soundtrack for the Tokyo-based film from the *Fast and Furious* franchise.

Best events
What to see

01 New Year shrine visit, citywide: The first visit of the year is known as *hatsumode*; millions flock to shrines all over Tokyo.
First week of January

02 Sumo, Kokugikan Sumo Stadium, Ryogoku: Thrice-yearly Grand Tournament with all the stars of Japan's national sport.
January, May, September, sumo.or.jp/en

03 Tokyo Marathon, citywide: Japanese love to run and this popular event is always over-subscribed.
February, tokyo42195.org

04 Tokyo Fashion Week, various venues: Biannual event showcasing mostly Japanese designers.
March and October, tokyo-mbfashionweek.com

05 Hanami, citywide: Citizens picnic under cherry trees across the city to mark the first blossoms of the year.
Late March to early April

06 Art Fair Tokyo, Tokyo International Forum: Annual contemporary-art fair, the largest of its kind in Japan.
Spring, artfairtokyo.com

07 Fireworks, Sumida River: *Hanabi*, or firework, have been a feature of Tokyo summers since the Edo period – this attracts one million people.
Last Saturday in July, sumidagawa-hanabi.com

08 Summer Sonic, Makuhari Messe: Three-day music festival split between Tokyo and Osaka, with big names from Japan and beyond.
August, summersonic.com

09 Tokyo International Film Festival, various venues: Tokyo's annual celebration of film, with a special focus on Japanese and Asian cinema.
October, tiff-jp.net

10 Tokyo Design Week, various venues: Annual citywide festival of design.
October, tokyodesignweek.jp

Rainy day
Weather-proof activities

01 Tokyo National Museum, Taito: Tokyo National Museum sits in Ueno Park alongside the National Museum for Western Art, the Tokyo Metropolitan Art Museum and Ueno Zoo. It has a superlative collection of Japanese and Asian art housed in several buildings, the most recent being the Gallery of Horyu-ji Treasures. Designed by Yoshio Taniguchi. it is home to a remarkable collection of artefacts from Nara's Horyu-ji Temple. Look out for the temporary exhibitions, too; they often feature rarely seen pieces from around Japan.
tnm.jp

02 Kabuki-za, Ginza: You can pass a drizzly afternoon watching *kabuki*, the 400-year-old dramatic art where all the parts are played by men. The costumes, make-up, music and stage settings are transporting and there are multiple intervals to ease you through what can be a five-hour marathon. Kabuki-za – the main venue for *kabuki* in Tokyo – first opened in 1889 and has been rebuilt several times. If you hear people shouting during the performance, don't be alarmed: they are calling out the stage names of the actors. The timing is crucial so it's best left to the experts. Lightweights can stick to one act and simultaneous translation is on offer.
kabuki-za.co.jp

03 Ghibli Museum, Mitaka: It helps if you know the cinematic works of Studio Ghibli but even if you haven't seen such classics as *Spirited Away* or *My Neighbor Totoro* you can still marvel at the brilliance of the best-known animation studio in Japan. Check for ticket availability – everyone loves this place.
ghibli-museum.jp

Sunny day
The great outdoors

01 Farmers' markets, citywide: Even city-dwellers love their farm-fresh produce and there are now several farmers' markets around Tokyo. Two are in the middle of the city: every weekend in front of the United Nations University (UNU) in Aoyama and the bigger Earth Day Market every month at Yoyogi Park. The UNU market is a short walk from Omotesando where, if you're not stocking up on fruit and veg, you can still enjoy quality nosh from several food trucks.
farmersmarket.jp; earthdaymarket.com

02 Rowing boats, Chidorigafuchi: Famous for its stunning cherry blossom in spring, Chidorigafuchi is the moat at the northwest of the Imperial Palace. You can rent a rowing or pedal boat from the boathouse. Take to the water in *sakura* season and you will avoid the crowds and be surrounded by pale-pink *somei-yoshino* and *kan-zakura* varieties. This spot gets top marks for romance.
2 Sanban-cho, Chiyoda-ku +81 (0)3 3234 1948

03 Yasukuni antiques market, Kudanshita: A Shinto shrine for the souls of 2.5 million war dead, Yasukuni is often spoken of in terms of political controversy but it is also a pleasant place for a stroll. The cherry blossom is particularly good and every Sunday it hosts a lively antiques market with more than 100 stalls. Nothing here is too pricey either – this is the place for vintage knick-knacks, pottery and curiosities. Another popular event is the Oedo antiques market, which is usually held on the first and third Sundays of the month at the Tokyo International Forum in Marunouchi.
yasukuni.or.jp

About Monocle
— Step inside

In 2007, Monocle was launched as a monthly magazine briefing on global affairs, business, culture, design and much more. We believed there was a globally minded audience of readers who were hungry for opportunities and experiences beyond their national borders.

Today Monocle is a complete media brand with print, audio and online elements – not to mention our expanding network of shops and cafés. Besides our London HQ we have seven international bureaux in Tokyo, Toronto, Istanbul, Singapore, New York, Zürich and Hong Kong. We continue to grow and flourish and at our core is the simple belief that there will always be a place for a print brand that is committed to telling fresh stories and sending photographers on assignments. It's also a case of knowing that our success is all down to the readers, advertisers and collaborators who have supported us along the way.

International bureau
Capital connections

MONOCLE's Tokyo bureau is an integral part of the operation, co-ordinating and commissioning our network of writers and correspondents across Asia. The office is headed up by Asia bureau chief Fiona Wilson, with support from Asia editor at large Kenji Hall, associate bureau chief Junichi Toyofuku and advertising executive Yasuhisa Ishikawa.

The editorial team are also regulars on our online radio station Monocle 24 and ensure that a steady stream of guests appear on our live shows, via the bureau's studio, to discuss everything from politics and business to food, drink and culture.

Online
Digital delivery

We also have a dynamic website: *monocle.com*. As well as being the place to hear Monocle 24, we use the site to present our films, which are beautifully shot and edited by our in-house team and provide a fresh perspective on our stories. Check out the films celebrating the cities that make up our Travel Guide Series before you explore the rest of the site.

Print
Committed to the page

MONOCLE is published 10 times a year. We have stayed loyal to our belief in quality print with two new seasonal publications: THE FORECAST, packed with key insights into the year ahead, and THE ESCAPIST, our summer travel-minded magazine. To sign up visit *monocle.com/subscribe*. Since 2013 we have also been publishing books, like this one, in partnership with Gestalten.

Home front
——
Our shop is on the same premises as our bureau

④
Retail and cafés
Good taste

Via our shops in Tokyo, Toronto, New York, Hong Kong, London and Singapore we sell products that cater to our readers' tastes and are produced in collaboration with brands we believe in. We also have cafés in Tokyo and London serving coffee and Japanese delicacies among other things – and we are set to expand this arm of our business.

⑤
Radio
Sound approach

Monocle 24 is our round-the-clock radio station that was launched in 2011. It delivers global news and shows covering foreign affairs, urbanism, business, culture, food and drink, design and print media. When you find yourself in Tokyo you can listen to our news programme, *The Globalist*, that is the perfect way to end the day; Monocle 24's editors, presenters and guests wrap up the agenda in international news and business. We also have a playlist to accompany you day and night, regularly assisted by live sessions that are hosted at our Midori House headquarters.

Join us

There are lots of ways to be part of the ever-expanding Monocle world whether in print, online, or on your radio. We'd love to have you join the club.

01
Read the magazine

You can buy Monocle magazine at newsstands in more than 60 countries around the world, or get yourself an annual subscription at *monocle.com.*

02
Listen to Monocle 24

You can tune in to Monocle 24 radio live via our free app, at *monocle.com* or on any internet-enabled radio. Or download our shows from iTunes or SoundCloud to keep informed as you travel the globe.

03
Subscribe to the Monocle Minute

Sign up today to the Monocle Minute, our free daily news and views email, at *monocle. com*. Our website is also where you'll find a world of free films, our online shop and updates about everything that we are up to.

MONOCLE

Keeping an eye and an ear on the world

Chief photographer
Kohei Take

Still life
David Sykes

Photographers
Alexis Armanet
Kenzaburo Fukuhara
Mika Ishikawa
Shinichi Ito
Tetsuya Ito
Norio Koga
Shoda Masahiro
Hayato Noge
Shigekazu Onuma
Madoka Sakamoto
Taro Terasawa
Keita Yamamoto
Keita Yasukawa

Images
Mitsumasa Fujitsuka
Gallery Koyanagi
Hideaki Kawashima (photo by
Kenji Takahashi, courtesy of
Tomio Koyama Gallery)
National Theatre of Japan
Takarazuka Revue

Writers
Dave Broom
W David Marx
Kenji Hall
Kenya Hara
David Karashima
Masamichi Katayama
Kunichi Nomura
Mark Robinson
Kaori Shoji
Richard Spencer Powell
Robbie Swinnerton
Junichi Toyofuku
Fiona Wilson

Illustrators
Satoshi Hashimoto
Tokuma
Masao Yamazaki

Monocle
EDITOR IN CHIEF & CHAIRMAN
Tyler Brûlé
EDITOR
Andrew Tuck
CREATIVE DIRECTOR
Richard Spencer Powell

**The Monocle Travel
Guide Series**
SERIES EDITOR
Joe Pickard
SENIOR SUB EDITOR
Amy Richardson
RESEARCHER/WRITER
Mikaela Aitken
DESIGNER
Sam Brogan
PHOTO EDITORS
*Matthew Beaman
Renee Melides
Shin Miura*
PRODUCTION
*Jacqueline Deacon
Dan Poole
Chloë Ashby
Sean McGeady
Sonia Zhuravlyova*

**The Monocle Travel Guide
Series: Tokyo**
GUIDE EDITOR
Fiona Wilson

ASSOCIATE EDITOR
Kenji Hall

DESIGNER
Jay Yeo

PHOTO EDITOR
Poppy Shibamoto

CHAPTER EDITING

Need to know
Kenji Hall

 Hotels
Fiona Wilson

Food and drink
*Kenji Hall
Jun Toyofuku
Fiona Wilson*

Retail
*Kenji Hall
Jun Toyofuku
Fiona Wilson*

Things we'd buy
Fiona Wilson

Essays
*Kenji Hall
Jun Toyofuku
Fiona Wilson*

Culture
Fiona Wilson

Design and architecture
Fiona Wilson

Sport and fitness
Kenji Hall

Walks
*Kenji Hall
Fiona Wilson*

Resources
*Kenji Hall
Fiona Wilson*

Research
Kentaro Harumiya
Keane Knapp
Alia Massoud
Marie-Sophie Schwarzer
Jeremy Toh
Junichi Toyofuku

Special thanks
Paul Fairclough
Nelly Gocheva
Maria Hamer
Keisuke Imaizumi
Yuki Inoue
Yasuhisa Ishikawa
Nao Kohara
Edward Lawrenson
Azusa Nakagawa
Lola Oduba
Ben Olsen
Atsushi Okahashi
Nanako Sato
Rebekah Wilson

The collection

We hope you have found the Monocle Travel Guide to Tokyo useful, inspiring and entertaining. There's plenty more to get your teeth into: see our suite of travel guides below. Buy them today at all good bookshops or visit the online stores at *monocle.com* and *shop.gestalten.com*.

01
London
The sights, sounds and style of the British capital.

02
New York
We get a taste for the best of the Big Apple.

03
Tokyo
Japan's capital in all its energetic, enigmatic glory.

04
Hong Kong
Get down to business in this dramatic city.

05
Madrid
A captivating city abuzz with spirit and adventure.

06
Bangkok
Stimulate your senses with the exotic and eclectic.

07
Istanbul
Where Asia and Europe meet – with thrilling results.

08
Miami
We unpack the Magic City's box of tricks.

09
Rio de Janeiro
An enchanting city of beaches and bossa nova.

10
Paris
Wander with us through the City of Light.

11
Singapore
Modernity meets tradition in the Garden City.

12
Vienna
Waltz your way through the Austrian capital.